Yuji Uesugi (Ed.)

Peacebuilding and Security Sector Governance in Asia

AF723357

Geneva Centre for the
Democratic Control of Armed Forces
(DCAF)

Hiroshima University Partnership Project
for Peacebuilding and Capacity Development
(HiPeC)

LIT

Peacebuilding and Security Sector Governance in Asia

edited by

Yuji Uesugi

LIT

This book is printed on acid-free paper.

Cover Picture: © derrrek / iStockphoto.com

The opinions expressed in this volume are those of the authors of individual chapters and do not necessarily reflect the opinions of the editor, or the institutional positions of either the Geneva Centre for the Democratic Control of Armed Forces (DCAF) or the Hiroshima University Partnership Project for Peacebuilding and Capacity Development (HiPeC). Neither DCAF nor HiPeC are responsible for either the views expressed or the accuracy of facts and other forms of information contained in this publication.

Bibliographic information published by the Deutsche Nationalbibliothek
The Deutsche Nationalbibliothek lists this publication in the Deutsche Nationalbibliografie; detailed bibliographic data are available in the Internet at http://dnb.d-nb.de.

ISBN 978-3-643-80169-2

A catalogue record for this book is available from the British Library

©LIT VERLAG GmbH & Co. KG Wien,
Zweigniederlassung Zürich 2014
Klosbachstr. 107
CH-8032 Zürich
Tel. +41 (0) 44-251 75 05
Fax +41 (0) 44-251 75 06
E-Mail: zuerich@lit-verlag.ch
http://www.lit-verlag.ch

LIT VERLAG Dr. W. Hopf
Berlin 2014
Fresnostr. 2
D-48159 Münster
Tel. +49 (0) 2 51-62 03 20
Fax +49 (0) 2 51-23 19 72
E-Mail: lit@lit-verlag.de
http://www.lit-verlag.de

Distribution:
In Germany: LIT Verlag Fresnostr. 2, D-48159 Münster
Tel. +49 (0) 2 51-620 32 22, Fax +49 (0) 2 51-922 60 99, E-mail: vertrieb@lit-verlag.de
In Austria: Medienlogistik Pichler-ÖBZ, e-mail: mlo@medien-logistik.at
In the UK: Global Book Marketing, e-mail: mo@centralbooks.com
In North America: International Specialized Book Services, e-mail: orders@isbs.com
e-books are available at www.litwebshop.de

Contents

Foreword

HIROSHIMA UNIVERSITY PARTNERSHIP PROJECT FOR PEACEBUILDING AND CAPACITY DEVELOPMENT (HiPeC)

Asia's long history and wide range of experiences in peace and conflict have created unique approaches to security that merit distinct investigation, and this is one of the main research features of the Hiroshima University Partnership Project for Peacebuilding and Capacity Development (HiPeC). This commitment is reflected in our support for one of our core project members, Professor Yuji Uesugi, and his proposal that the main workshop for the book project "Peacebuilding and Security Sector Governance in Asia" be held in August 2010 in Hiroshima under the auspices of the HiPeC-II (2010-13) research agenda. The very lively discussion of that workshop inspired not only the contributors of this volume, but also the HiPeC researchers, who were prompted to establish two new active research offices in the conflict-affected areas of Nepal and the Philippines as a result.

If we understand peacebuilding as the human endeavour to prevent the recurrence of conflict, then it must also be understood as the art of creating trust and building confidence. Through history the Asian peoples have developed their own ways of making peace and providing security through the experiences of different communities, and they have striven to preserve them, even under the strains of Western colonisation. The post-Cold War era revealed the very simple fact that almost all conflicts originate at the local level, a fact which emphasises the proper and legitimate role that indigenous initiatives have to play in solving conflict and securing peace.

in Asia as it is in other regions. At the same time, many authors are careful to underline that external actors have an important role to play in supporting national initiatives, whether by providing technical expertise, or facilitating dialogue, knowledge-sharing and the exchange of ideas, at either national or regional levels. Facilitating regional dialogue of the kind that has resulted in this collection fits well within the mission of the Geneva Centre for the Democratic Control of Armed Forces (DCAF).

It would not have been possible to complete this volume without the invaluable support of a number of institutions and individuals. DCAF thus wishes to thank the Hiroshima University Partnership Project for Peacebuilding and Capacity Development (HiPeC) for their excellent collaboration throughout this project, and the Bangkok-based Institute of Security and International Studies (ISIS) for their impeccable organisation of the second authors' workshop. We are grateful to DCAF colleagues Edward Burger, Yury Korobovsky, Eleanor Pavey and Kathrin Reed for their assistance at various stages of the project. Special thanks go to Fairlie Chappuis whose crucial role in the review and editing process has significantly shaped the project from its inception. Finally, we would like to acknowledge the excellent work of the editor, Professor Yuji Uesugi, and thank all of the volume's contributors from whom we have learned a vast amount. It has been a privilege to work with people so committed to telling the often difficult and sensitive stories of the security sector, its governance and reform in Asia.

Heiner Hänggi
Assistant Director and Head of Research, DCAF

support to SSR in Afghanistan. Other organisations use a broad understanding of SSR that encompasses a wide range of actors, i.e., including statutory institutions and non-statutory actors, as well as security actors and their civilian oversight mechanisms. For example, the Development Assistance Committee (DAC) of the Organisation for Economic Co-operation and Development (OECD) put forward a widely used definition, which describes the security sector in terms of two pillars: (a) the security forces; and (b) the civilian bodies responsible for their oversight and control. This definition encompasses: state institutions, which have a formal mandate to ensure the safety of the state and its citizens against acts of violence and coercion (e.g. the armed forces, the police and civil defence forces, the intelligence services, and similar bodies; judicial and penal institutions), and elected, duly appointed, and/or hereditary civil authorities responsible for control and oversight (e.g. the judiciary, the legislature, and the executive, including its associated line ministries, etc.).[9]

Adopting the OECD/DAC's definition, a broad and comprehensive approach to SSR includes the following four security sector quadrants: (1) statutory security actors; (2) formal oversight mechanisms; (3) civil society actors; and (4) non-statutory security providers (See Figure 1).[10] If in reality current efforts at SSR do not necessarily encompass such a comprehensive approach, this study adopts this view because it provides a wide-angle lens, allowing for a holistic picture of the SSG in Asia to emerge.

Other important features of this comprehensive approach can be represented as "one approach, two principles and three dimensions".[11] "One approach" refers to the importance of local/national ownership as a principle for external actors, whose role ought to remain that of assisting a host government and society to improve the legitimate functions of their security sector. "Two principles" refers to (i) the central goal of improving the effectiveness of security provision and oversight, as well as (ii) their accountability to the people. This emphasis on accountability plays an important role in linking SSR to democratic governance.

Figure 1: Four Security Sector Quadrants[12]

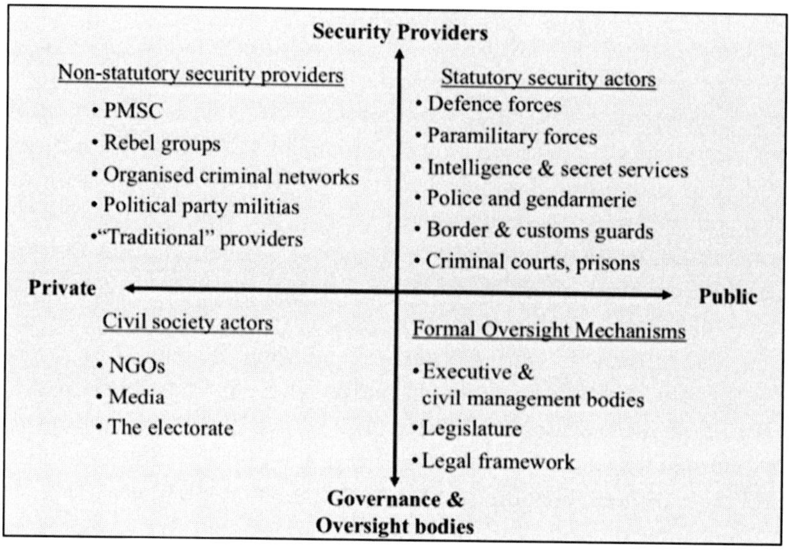

Finally, "three dimensions" refers to the fact that the needs of the security sector must be addressed in their holistic, technical, and political dimensions. The holistic nature of SSR is represented in Figure 2. Technical dimensions refer to the wide range of expertise SSR requires: for example, police reform may require technical experts in forensics, criminal psychology, or crowd control, among many other areas.

Furthermore, a common feature of SSR in Asia (as elsewhere) is its political nature, since SSR always involves a power struggle amongst political stakeholders. While keeping in mind the holistic nature of SSR and the significance of its technical dimensions, this study will primarily highlight the political dimension of changes in SSG by focusing on the political aspect of the challenges, rather than on the assessment of technical requirements. This is because political analysis is critical to an accurate understanding of the context in which SSR may be carried out, but is often neglected in the existing literature.

Figure 2: Holistic Nature of SSR[13]

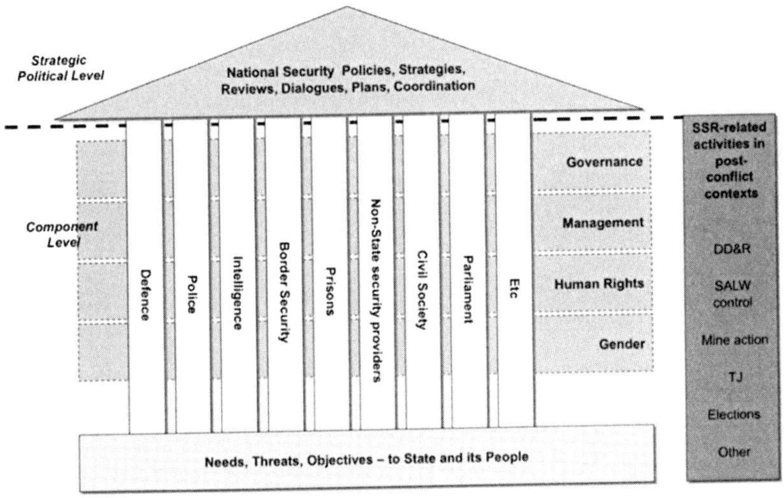

The security sector of a state provides one of the most fundamental public goods – public safety as well as law and order – through the monopoly of violence, which can be regarded as a core function of a modern state apparatus.[14] Hence, changes in the security sector, which may lead to political and social transformation, can create anxiety among the political elite in the host society. The political nature of SSR should not be underestimated in order to maintain harmony between two possibly conflicting themes: local/national ownership and democratic governance in the context of nascent democracy.

Nonetheless, in reality, such a comprehensive approach to SSR, with an emphasis on its political nature, has barely materialised. This is partly because there are numerous political and technical constraints to implementing such an agenda, but also partly because there is a deficit of adequate human resources, as well as a lack of proper policy approaches and methodology. Moreover, because of its proximity to the power centre of a state, SSR often faces resistance and generates anxiety among the political elite and military leadership if external actors attempt to enforce a certain model or standard of SSG. Such uneasiness on the part of the political elite and military leadership can easily be anticipated in countries with a strong state apparatus or with a legacy of significant military involvement in politics, such as Indonesia, the Philippines, Thailand, Nepal, Sri Lanka, and Timor-Leste.

With regard to political sensitivity, consideration over the use of the term 'reform' deserves more than passing attention. While external actors have a tendency to call their efforts to support the security sector of a recipient state a mode of 'reform', some host governments are reluctant to recognise such an undertaking as 'reform' and prefer to call it something else: for example, development, transformation, or reconstruction. Hence, some advocates and practitioners of SSR avoid using the term 'reform' in order to prevent unnecessary resistance emerging within a host government when advocating for SSR. However, the focus of this study is turned towards improving SSG not for these negative reasons, but rather because it is only through promoting effective and accountable SSG – a key element of human security – that states can address their security challenges successfully.

A Typology of SSG in the Context of Peacebuilding

SSG Tasks in Peacebuilding

A close analysis of SSG in the cases presented in this volume suggests that tasks associated with improving SSG fall into two broad categories: (1) political transition/democratisation and (2) post-conflict state-building. Of course, most post-conflict state-building endeavours also aspire to political transition/democratisation, even if political transition/democratisation efforts may lead to tension and ultimately violent conflict in a society if they are handled inappropriately. It is likely that these two types of tasks overlap in their objectives and activities, and thus may be very closely linked in their actual implementation on the ground. Nonetheless, they are presented here separately for analytical clarity.

(1) Political transition/democratisation. The first category includes attempts to enhance SSG in the process of political transition and democratisation. SSR is closely related to, if not an integral part of, a wider political reform in the system of political power. The primary features and challenges of SSG in Indonesia, the Philippines, and Thailand, for example, fall into this category. Although Indonesia, the Philippines, and Thailand have dealt with rebellion or insurgency in Aceh, Mindanao, and the Southern region respectively, their armed struggles have been confined to certain parts within each country's territories. The fundamental tasks of SSR in those countries are closely

linked with the process of a wider political transition and democratisation and include (i) redefining the relationship between the political elite and the statutory security forces; (ii) the professionalisation and de-politicisation of statutory security forces; and (iii) strengthening the democratic/civilian control of the security forces.

(2) Post-conflict state-building. The other category of SSG tasks relates to the challenges common in the aftermath of violent armed conflict. The main features of SSG in Nepal, Sri Lanka, and Timor-Leste fall into this category. Despite the fact that these countries had different patterns of conflict termination and different degrees of external involvement, they face similar challenges in post-conflict state-building.

The Nepalese ended their conflict with a peace agreement, which set out a regime change and a new power-sharing arrangement among the former adversaries, including the integration of statutory armed forces and non-statutory forces, with lukewarm support from the international community and interference from neighbouring countries. In contrast, a protracted civil war in Sri Lanka was terminated through a military victory of the incumbent government, which does not recognise the necessity of a drastic overhaul of its security sector, nor does it have sufficient political will to change the fundamental character of the state apparatus. Timor-Leste distinguishes itself from these two cases as an exemplary case of post-conflict state-building, with massive external involvement, that was carried out after a successful secession (or restoration of independence). The United Nations assumed transitional executive authority, including the role of providing justice and law enforcement over the territory of Timor-Leste, and, further, undertook executive policing in Timor-Leste due to a lack of local capacity. This was not the case in Nepal and Sri Lanka, where effective and functioning armed forces were able to perform these tasks.

Case Study Summaries

(1) Political Transition/Democratisation

Indonesia	A series of difficult negotiations ended a violent conflict in Aceh, which was fought between the Government of Indonesia and the anti-government group, the Free Aceh Movement (GAM). A memorandum of understanding (MoU) signed in August 2005 allowed Aceh to be rebuilt as a province of Indonesia, while Indonesia as a state underwent a political transition from authoritarian rule to democracy. SSR has been carried out under strong local initiative and as a part of larger efforts at political reform. The presence of external actors, including those assisting in post-tsunami recovery in Aceh, also contributed to support for the implementation of the MoU. In Aceh, after the signing of the MoU, the majority of the members of the GAM returned home safely and were accepted by their communities, with little evidence of tension between GAM members, their communities, the military, the police, or the local government. In many cases, GAM members were welcomed back as heroes. Most displaced people also returned to their villages and homes. The security situation in Aceh has improved significantly since then, so that people now enjoy freedom of movement. Following the signing of the MoU, two local elections for the governorship of Aceh were held peacefully in 2006 and in 2012. It is safe to say that political reconciliation between the Government of Indonesia and the former members of the GAM was promoted as a result of a series of political developments in Aceh.

Philippines	The Government of the Philippines has faced conflict with several Islamic insurgency groups, such as the Moro National Liberation Front (MNLF) and the Moro Islamic Liberation Front (MILF) in Mindanao. While a series of peace talks between the government and MNLF led to the creation of the Autonomous Region in Muslim Mindanao, the violence continued between the government and the MILF. Thus, the armed forces of the Philippines were being reformed as a part of a wider political transition and democratisation process, while at the same time conducting counterinsurgency operations in Mindanao. The signing of peace agreements between the government and anti-government groups, such as the MNLF and the Communist Party of the Philippines' New People's Army (CPP-NPA) in 1996 and 2000, respectively, constituted a key milestone for initiating a series of efforts in SSG, as the lack of a peace agreement had undermined serious SSG efforts, especially in the case of conflict between the government and the MILF. Nevertheless, a failure to incorporate a proper mechanism for dealing with non-state armed groups in the peace agreement threatened its implementation. Allegations of government failure to implement the peace agreement led to the emergence of breakaway factions, which further complicated the challenges of SSG in the Philippines. The recent peace agreement between the government and the MILF will serve as a test of political reconciliation between the government and armed groups in Mindanao.

Thailand	Thailand faces a rebellion of the Muslim minority in the Deep South, which is closely linked with a political struggle in the power centre that involves the statutory security actors. Political violence in Bangkok in 2010 reflected the tensions prevalent in Thailand as it undergoes a political transition to democracy under a constitutional monarchy. A delicate triangular relationship between the monarchy, the military, and democratic forces will have to be addressed, though it may prove too sensitive for domestic actors to undertake, but too intrusive for external actors to engage. The conflict in the Deep South has received the most attention in Thailand due to its connection to issues of terrorism, but it is in fact more accurately understood as a reflection of a much larger challenge to Thailand's political power structure. To address the violent conflict in the Deep South, the government established the National Reconciliation Commission in March 2005, but little progress resulted from this step due to much wider power struggles at the centre. In fact, it was the Council for National Security, established as a result of the coup in September 2006, that abrogated the most democratic 1997 Constitution. The 2007 election marked the beginning of a rivalry between the so-called 'Yellow Shirts' and 'Red Shirts', which erupted into violence in 2010. While a Truth and Reconciliation Commission, a Committee on Reform Strategy, a Committee on Reform Assembly, and a Fact-finding Committee were established, the fate of political reconciliation between the belligerents of the 2010 political conflict in fact depends heavily on much broader processes of social and political change in Thailand.

(2) Post-conflict State-building

Nepal	The violent conflict between the Government of Nepal and the Communist Party of Nepal (the so-called Maoists) was terminated with a comprehensive peace agreement, which inaugurated a difficult process of regime change from monarchy to democracy. A new power-sharing arrangement among the former adversaries, which led to a deadlock in the political transition, has undermined SSG in Nepal, despite the fact that it received support from the international community and the effective and functional armed forces loyal to the former King. Political actors are still negotiating the principles of the future structures of the state and the democratic system of governance inside the elected Constituent Assembly, which abolished the monarchy at its first sitting in May 2008. They will have to find a way to accommodate the contradictory ideologies of royalists, communists, and pluralists within a new framework of statehood. Bringing justice to the victims of armed conflict is an entry point for SSR and is an integral part of peacebuilding. The significance of SSG in political and social reconciliation has been contextualised amidst negotiation over future state structures and systems of governance. The peace agreements have identified, in principle, the need to redesign the security sector and have provisions for the "democratisation of Nepal Army", "integration and rehabilitation" of the People's Liberation Army (the armed wing of the Maoists), and "inclusive structures of security agencies", but the process of implementation remains subject to negotiation, which has yet to happen.

Sri Lanka	A protracted violent conflict between the Government of Sri Lanka and the anti-government group, the Liberation Tigers of Tamil Eelam (LTTE), which sought secession from Sri Lanka to establish an independent Tamil state in the northern and the eastern parts of the country, divided communities and social structures. After a series of unsuccessful attempts to settle the armed conflict through peace talks, it was finally terminated in May 2009 with a military victory by the government. This victory resulted in the consolidation of majority rule, with some elements of nation-building and national reconciliation included on the agenda of peacebuilding and SSG. Sri Lanka has very effective security institutions, together with a strong executive body, but its inherent peacebuilding and SSG challenges concern the lack of accountability and legitimacy of the government in the eyes of the Tamil minority. The comprehensive defeat of the LTTE has to a great extent removed the pressure on the government from anti-government, non-statutory forces and has thus provided various stakeholders with an opportunity for reconciliation and nation-building within the framework of the security sector overhaul. For instance, new recruitment schemes that focus on minority communities could be introduced, as the current composition of the armed forces is not ethnically representative. However, the sudden removal of pressure did not automatically shift prevailing attitudes and policy toward the security sector, as threats and threat perceptions still continue to dominate.

Timor-Leste	After a violent secession from Indonesia in 1999, Timor-Leste has undertaken the development of SSG with massive external involvement. For example, the United Nations assumed transitional executive authority, including the role of providing justice and law enforcement over the territory of Timor-Leste, before the restoration of independence in May 2002. Yet, even after Timor-Leste gained its independence, SSR was led by external actors, such as the United Nations, who continued executive policing while carrying out capacity building for the National Police Force, while other bilateral donors supported the reform of the defence forces. Despite this external support towards the Timorese security sector, Timor-Leste experienced a crisis in 2006 caused by the lack of capacity and integrity of local security actors. In Timor-Leste, society was not divided in terms of religion or ethnicity, but people were divided between different political orientations because they experienced several armed conflicts, such as the independence struggle against the Portuguese and later against Indonesia's forced annexation. The crisis that erupted immediately after the referendum in 1999 gave birth to a new state with a new constitution in 2002. The Commission for Reception, Truth and Reconciliation was introduced to facilitate social reconciliation between victims and perpetrators. Nevertheless, underlying social divisions persisted and also became prevalent among members of the security forces in Timor-Leste, which were manipulated by competing factions within the political elite, causing a major crisis in the security sector in 2006. The results of the presidential and parliamentary elections of 2007 and 2012 seem to indicate that political reconciliation has been achieved to a degree that makes further violence unlikely.

Key Issues in SSG in Peacebuilding

This study introduces a typology of SSG in the context of peacebuilding in order to elucidate the nexus between SSG and peacebuilding. A close analysis of major cases in Asia has illuminated a conceptual framework that is useful for understanding the features and challenges of SSG in the region. The framework includes the following four key issues: (1) political reconciliation; (2) legitimacy of the government; (3) civil-military relations; and (4) civilian oversight mechanisms for democratic governance.

(1) Political Reconciliation. The first key issue is political reconciliation among former belligerents, which can be institutionalised in the form of a peace agreement, democratic constitution, and/or transitional justice mechanisms, such as a truth and reconciliation commission. All cases examined in this study have experienced violent internal strife or insurgency in pursuit of either secession or regime change, and each generated a different pattern of conflict termination. It is expected that a diligent effort towards SSR and more effective SSG will promote political reconciliation among former belligerents as well as social reconciliation between perpetrators and victims, thus contributing to strengthening national unity.

Violent conflicts in Indonesia, the Philippines, and Thailand have to be resolved, in principle, in a peace agreement between the government and anti-government elements against a backdrop of a much larger process of socio-political transformation and democratisation at the state level. For example, in the cases of Aceh and Mindanao, a series of peace talks and the signing of peace agreements between the government and the anti-government groups, such as GAM and MNLF, constituted key milestones for initiating a series of efforts to improve SSG in both cases. At the same time, because anti-government groups will have to find a way to achieve or accommodate their aspirations within a framework of a more democratic unitary state, the issue of political reconciliation becomes equally significant for SSR in political transition. Furthermore, the case of Thailand illustrates the necessity for political reconciliation among political powers in the centre before any meaningful reform in the security sector can take place.

In the case of post-conflict state-building, in which a new form of statehood is more likely to be pursued as a result of conflict termination, unless local stakeholders achieve a consensus vision for the state, it is difficult to have a clear sense of direction for any attempt at SSR. The issue of political reconciliation was particularly acute in the case of Nepal, where the conflict was terminated through peace talks, resulting in a power-sharing arrangement between former belligerents. Although a comprehensive peace agreement was signed in Nepal, which stipulated provisions for integration and rehabilitation of the Maoist Army and democratisation of the Nepal Army, the fact that the parties were unable to agree on the constitution undermined the process of SSR. The issue of political reconciliation between the majority government and the minority group is equally important in Sri Lanka, where the violent conflict was ended by the government in a unilateral military victory. Moreover, the 2006 security sector crisis in Timor-Leste demonstrates vividly the importance of political reconciliation for a nascent democracy whose security sector remains fragile and susceptible to political interference.

(2) Legitimacy of the Government. The second key issue is the legitimacy of the government, especially in the eyes of minorities and/or marginalised groups. The presence of a legitimate government allows for democratic governance and civilian control of the security sector, which play a pivotal role in safeguarding effective and accountable SSG. The maturity of SSG in each country can serve as a barometer that measures the legitimacy of the government in the eyes of minorities and/or marginalised groups. SSR can be a vehicle for both promoting and damaging the legitimacy of the government, as statutory security forces often perform their duties at the interface between the government and the people.

The legitimacy of the government in the eyes of the people affects popular support for the statutory security forces. Although this issue has not been addressed explicitly in the case studies of this volume, the relationship between the government and minority groups over the question of whether or not a minority group can embrace its central and local governments as legitimate can influence SSG in countries in political transition – as, for example, in Indonesia's Aceh, the Philippines' Mindanao, and Thailand's Deep South. For this reason, efforts to make the society concerned more pluralistic and democratic, such that the rights and aspirations of minority groups can be safeguarded, provide a good barometer of SSG in these countries.

This point was equally true for the case of Sri Lanka, whose police and armed forces were considered to be professional, effective, and accountable for the majority of its population – Sinhalese – while the same institutions were viewed with suspicion on the part of the Tamil minority. Tamils, for example, felt that the very state security forces that had often threatened the human security of Tamil people would not protect their interests. This demonstrates how the legitimacy of the government can be threatened if the state security forces lack broad integrity. By the same token, no matter how professional Sri Lanka's police and armed forces are, their integrity in the eyes of the minority cannot be improved as long as the legitimacy of the government is in question. In contrast, in Timor-Leste, a serious mistake was made during the transition phase, when the United Nations recruited officers for the newly established police force from among the former Indonesian police, while many veterans, who had devoted their lives to the liberation struggle, were side-lined in the post-conflict state-building process. This legacy, together with the lack of popular support for the police, has continued to undermine the legitimacy of the government in Timor-Leste since its independence in 2002.

(3) Civil-Military Relations. The third key issue is civil-military relations. SSR in Asia cannot be understood without appreciating the roles of security forces, especially that of the military, in politics and in wider society. In other words, SSR is heavily influenced by prevailing civil-military relations in any context, and because the armed forces of most of the countries examined in this volume have a history of considerable involvement in the socio-political affairs of the country, SSR in these countries is determined to a great extent by the relationship between the government and the statutory security forces. Hence, redefining civil-military relations is a core activity of SSR. This is extremely difficult, though, when the military maintains a vested interest in its position in politics.

Continuing localised conflicts in Aceh, Mindanao, and the Deep South have affected the civil-military relations at the power centres in Indonesia, the Philippines, and Thailand, respectively, as these countries undergo political transitions and confront their legacies of military involvement in politics. In Thailand, which experienced its 18th coup in September 2006, the role of the King in politics, together with his ties to the armed forces, has complicated civil-military relations. And the fact that counterinsurgency operations were carried out in these conflict areas by security forces has allowed them to maintain certain leverage and influence over politics.

Because of the long-standing involvement of the military in socio-political affairs in Thailand, it is very difficult for any structure of civil-military relations to develop in such a way as to enable meaningful SSR. In the Philippines, the continuing use of the military in domestic conflict and internal security has undermined democratic civil-military relations, of which the institutional and functional separation of the police from the military is a central feature. Nevertheless, although the constitutional and legal frameworks for democratic civil-military relations exist, including not only the institutional and functional separation of the police from the military, but also the primacy of civilian authority over the military at all times and the legal subjugation of the military to civilian control, the military continues to exert substantive influence on politics due to its continuing role in counterinsurgency in conflict areas, where coercion remains salient to regime survival in the face of threats of secession from armed anti-government elements. In contrast, the end of armed conflict in Aceh created a window of opportunity to end excessive military influence in politics and thereby to allow SSG in Indonesia to develop in the right direction.

In the post-conflict state-building context, civil-military relations are central to SSG challenges, although the nature of the challenges differs among the cases examined in this volume. In Nepal, the situation is quite complicated because the Nepalese Army (which used to serve the King) and the revolutionary army are being integrated in the absence of a clear vision of statehood and consensus on the type of new armed forces. The key challenges of SSG in Nepal thus involve the transformation of the identity, roles, and functions of its army, as well as the redefinition of civil-military relations. In Sri Lanka, statutory forces wiped out the anti-government forces, and the democratically elected government assumed supreme control over the military. Thus, the key challenge for SSG was not so much constituting democratic civil-military relations, but rather generating trust of minorities in public institutions, such as the military, that had previously served as the oppressive machinery of the majority-led state. This challenge was complicated further, given that state-led discrimination continued to exist in the eyes of the minorities. The government will have to address this issue and establish 'peacetime' civil-military relations. In Timor-Leste, the crisis of 2006 showed that the central challenge of SSG was not excessive interference of the military in politics, but rather how to break off illegal and patrimonial relationships between politicians and security actors.

(4) Civilian Oversight Mechanisms for Democratic Governance. The fourth key issue is the presence of functioning civilian oversight mechanisms. In order to increase the accountability and integrity of security forces, it is essential that effective and accountable civilian oversight mechanisms be established so that they can serve as the gatekeepers of democratic governance of the security forces. The major challenge of SSR in Asia can be attributed to the underdevelopment of such mechanisms. While it is necessary to develop formal, institutional, and legal bases for civilian oversight, this volume highlights the importance of providing sufficient attention to informal and cultural aspects of civilian oversight. The effectiveness of civilian oversight mechanisms depends partly on the quality and political maturity of the civilian leadership, as SSR can infringe upon the vested (but illegitimate) interests of, and, thus, can give rise to serious anxiety with, the political elite in a post-conflict society.

In countries in political transition, formal civilian oversight mechanisms for democratic governance of the security sector have remained largely ineffective. An essential lack of relevant capacities and the political will to utilise civilian oversight mechanisms has hampered the development of effective democratic control over the security sector. Despite the fact that various civilian oversight institutions were established in executive, legislative, judicial, and quasi-judicial apparatuses in the Philippines, for example, they have either misused or abused their oversight functions such that members of the security forces have committed human rights violations with impunity. Similarly, despite the existence of a formal right to scrutinise defence policy, the Thai parliament stands without sufficient capacity in military and security affairs to effectively monitor SSG. In sharp contrast, civilian oversight mechanisms in Indonesia, including the media and civil society organisations, began to function in name and in reality, leading to public disclosure of military 'sanctuaries', which has contributed to progress and wider democratisation in the country.

In Nepal, where the process of writing the new constitution has been deadlocked and the legal frameworks are too weak, it became challenging to establish effective civilian oversight mechanisms. The negotiation process over the agendas of civilian control and oversight of the security forces as well as the future of the People's Liberation Army has remained at a standstill as a result of divergent threat perceptions among national political actors and regional neighbours, in particular India. In Sri Lanka, almost all security sector bodies have been legitimised through legislation enacted by parliament. Because of the armed conflict with the LTTE, however, parliament allowed the president to control the direction of security policy. Likewise, in the face of continuing armed conflict, the legal system and the judiciary have come under severe criticism for corruption, politicisation, and inefficiency, and they have become dysfunctional. The United Nations installed democratic civilian oversight mechanisms in Timor-Leste, but political elites effectively undermined these mechanisms to the extent that the prime minister, who is democratically elected, now has considerable influence over decision-making in parliament, the ministry of defence and security, and other civilian oversight institutions.

Structure of the Volume

This volume has eight chapters, including the Introduction, which has laid out the theoretical underpinnings of this study and their significance. Based on the typology of SSG that is articulated here, the main body of this study is divided into two parts: (1) political transition/democratisation and (2) post-conflict state-building. In the first part, the cases of Indonesia (Chapter 1), the Philippines (Chapter 2), and Thailand (Chapter 3) will be examined. In the second part, the cases of Nepal (Chapter 4), Sri Lanka (Chapter 5), and Timor-Leste (Chapter 6) will be discussed. The concluding chapter will present a set of reflections drawn from a close examination of the six case studies and it will intend to promote further discussion of SSG in Asia.

Notes

1 This book project was launched in 2010. Since then, many developments were witnessed in the security sector of the countries examined in the book. Although the authors of this volume tried their best to incorporate such developments in their manuscripts wherever possible, the case studies of this volume are in principle based on their analysis of the situation in 2010-11.

2 See further: "Hiroshima University Partnership Project for Peacebuilding and Capacity Development", http://home.hiroshima-u.ac.jp/hipec/

3 ASSET is a professional association of education and training organisations and institutions that support the development of SSR capacity within governments, donors, security sector institutions, parliaments, civil society organisations, and international/regional organisations. See further: http://asset-ssr.org/

4 DCAF is an international foundation, established in 2000 on the initiative of Switzerland, whose mission is to contribute to enhancing security sector governance (SSG) through security sector reform (SSR). The Centre combines conceptual, analytical, and operational capabilities in order to support the international community in pursuing a holistic SSG/SSR agenda. The DCAF Foundation Council currently comprises over sixty member states and several permanent observers, including, among others, Indonesia, the Philippines, and Thailand. See further: http://www.dcaf.ch/

5 United Nations, General Assembly and Security Council, *Report of the Panel on United Nations Peace Operations*, A/55/305-S/2000/809, 21 August 2000, para. 13.

6 *Ibid.*

7 *Security Sector Governance and Reform*, DCAF Backgrounder 05/2009 (Geneva: Geneva Centre for the Democratic Control of Armed Forces: 2009), p. 1.

8 It is surely debatable whether or not all countries examined in this study have failed to provide security and justice to their peoples. However, it is not the intention of this study to argue what would constitute a failed or fragile state, but rather to present a comparative study of developments in SSG within selected countries in Southeast Asia and South Asia.

9 *Handbook on Security System Reform: Supporting Security and Justice*, 2007 Edition (Paris: Organisation for Economic Co-operation and Development – OECD, 2007), pp. 105-106, http://www.oecd.org/dataoecd/43/25/38406485.pdf.

10 David M. Law, *The Post-Conflict Security Sector*, Policy Paper No. 14 (Geneva: Geneva Centre for the Democratic Control of Armed Forces: 2006), p. 17.

11 *Ibid.*

12 *SSR in a Nutshell. Manual for Introductory Training on Security Sector Reform* (Geneva: Geneva Centre for the Democratic Control of Armed Forces/ International Security Sector Advisory Team: 2011), p. 7.

13 *Ibid.*, p. 11.

14 Anthony Giddens, *The Nation-State and Violence* (Berkley and Los Angeles: University of California Press, 1981), pp. 7-34.

Part I:

Political Transition / Democratisation

1 *Democratisation, Peace Processes and Security Sector Governance in Indonesia: The Case of Aceh*

SAMSU RIZAL PANGGABEAN

In the elections for the governorship of Aceh on 9 April 2012, Irwandi Yusuf, the governor from 2007 to 2011, lost to Zaini Abdullah and Muzakir Manaf, who became the new governor and deputy governor, respectively. Abdullah was the foreign minister of the now defunct Free Aceh Movement, or GAM, and Manaf was the commander of GAM's military wing. They stood for the Party of Aceh, a local political party. After the elections, Yusuf, who ran as an independent candidate, filed an appeal to the Indonesian Constitutional Court in Jakarta, accusing Abdullah's and Manaf's supporters of using violence and intimidation to win the elections. The Constitutional Court inspected the case and overturned the appeal. According to its Chief, the appeal was "baseless and unproven"; Yusuf, also a former rebel leader, accepted the ruling and congratulated the winner.[1]

Direct elections are the most important political event in Aceh since the peace-deal between the Government of Indonesia and the GAM in August 2005. The agreement, called the Memorandum of Understanding (MoU), stipulates the importance of free and fair local elections for peacebuilding. In the elections of 2012, there were 3,244,680 eligible voters in Aceh, and 75.73 per cent of them visited 9,786 voting booths to cast their votes on the election day. This level of participation was higher than the average level of electoral participation at the national level. Five pairs of candidates ran for the governorship and 137 pairs for district head positions in 17 districts. These candidates ran on national and local political party platforms and as independents. Many of these candidates were affiliated to

GAM, who competed among themselves and with candidates from civil society, technocratic, and other backgrounds.

The importance of post-conflict elections for peace and security in Aceh is obvious. Elections reinforce "the transition from warfare to politics"[2] and "from war to democracy".[3] Elections effectively include former rebels in the political process. In addition, elections play key roles in "managing political competition amongst Aceh's local elites, and providing the basis for good governance and effective development policy in Aceh".[4] Elections also concern another former party to the conflict in Aceh: members of the Indonesian police, assisted by the local military, have exercised their neutrality in all elections since 2005, including the 2012 local elections, by providing security during voting and by guarding the ballot boxes. The police and the military in post-conflict Aceh are no longer repressive institutions. The police, however, face the challenge of dealing with electoral violence and other sources of insecurity originating from former combatants.

This chapter is about how democratisation and the peace process have transformed the security sector governance (SSG) of Indonesia with special reference to the case of Aceh. Democratisation refers to the process of opening up political space, including improvements in contestation, participation, and human rights.[5] SSG refers to "the structures, processes, values and attitudes that shape decisions about security".[6] By treating democratisation and the peace process as causes of reforms in the security sector and not as entry points for security sector reform (SSR) programming, it explores two questions: First, to what extent did democratisation in post-Suharto Indonesia contribute to the peace process in Aceh? Second, to what extent did the peace process in Aceh transform SSG in the province?

Democratisation and SSR

The origin of SSR in Indonesia can be traced to the last year of the New Order under President Suharto and to the demands raised by the protest movement in different parts of the country. Clashes between protesters and the security forces of the New Order shook the country and in several cities led to the largest riots in the history of modern Indonesia, including in Jakarta, Medan, Solo, and other cities. These demands included abolishing the dual function doctrine (*dwifungsi*) of the armed forces, decentralisation of government, and ending corruption, collusion, and nepotism (or *Korupsi*, *Kolusi*, and *Nepotisme*, known by the acronym KKN). The armed forces, which included the police, were the backbone of the New Order, and their deep involvement in politics was justified by the *dwifungsi* doctrine. As one of the central demands of the protest movement, the abolition of the *dwifungsi* challenged the legitimacy of the New Order, as it was the most important source of distortion in the security sector.

Reformasi, the term used in Indonesia to describe the transition from authoritarianism to democracy, removed many obstacles to reform of the security sector. Former President Suharto, who had created the New Order and who had led it for more than three decades, persuaded himself and others of the efficacy of the regime; it was personally difficult for him to admit the mistakes of his regime. Therefore, when President Suharto stepped down in May 1998, the protests succeeded not only in toppling the regime, but also in removing a major obstacle toward reform of the security sector. The security forces – the steel frame of the New Order – initially tried to suppress the protests, but, in the end, they were unable to block the course of the transition and subsequent reforms. Eventually, the security forces had to face the fact that their future role in the country depended on joining the *reformasi* movement instead of maintaining the failing regime at all costs.

Reformasi, therefore, marked the end of certain functions, programmes, policies, and organisations inherited from the previous regime. Furthermore, although the politics of the first years of *reformasi* were chaotic and crisis-ridden, a strategic environment for reforms was created in the country. In the words of Harold Crouch, "the crisis was so severe that most of the surviving members of the New Order elite were persuaded that in order to save themselves they would have to accept substantial reforms, even when such reforms harmed the immediate interests of that elite itself".[7] President B.J. Habibie, in power from May 1998 until October 1999, capitalised on these conditions in a way that surprised many: he immediately released political prisoners, freed the media, allowed the formation of new political parties, and prepared the first free election in Indonesia since 1955. He also took a dramatic course of action by disengaging from East Timor.

The military adjusted itself according to the new situation. First, in September 1998 it produced a paper, "The New Paradigm of the

Armed Forces of Indonesia", which stated its readiness to relinquish many of its political and social roles. For the first time since 1971, the military promised to remain neutral during elections, severing its long link with the *Golongan Karya* (Golkar) party, the ruling party during the New Order period. The military dissolved its social and political affairs branch, an organisation used by the military to control civilian activities, including political parties, the media, and social organisations.[8] Other important measures taken by the military included withdrawing military officers holding positions in government and the bureaucracy as well as reducing, and ultimately removing, military representation in parliament.

The next phase of reforms came during the presidencies of Abdurrahman Wahid (1999 - 2001) and Megawati Sukarnoputri (2001-2004), mostly through legislation. In 2000, the People's Consultative Assembly (*Majelis Permusyawaratan Rakyat* – MPR) produced two important decrees: one on the separation of the police from the armed forces and the other on the roles and functions of the military and the police. These decrees serve as the conceptual foundation of military reform, civil-military relations, and other aspects of SSR. In 2002, during the presidency of Megawati, the parliament adopted the Law on National Defence and the Law on the National Police. In 2004, the parliament passed the Law on the new National Armed Forces of Indonesia (*Tentara Nasional Indonesia* – TNI).[9]

This legislation formalised the separation of the police from the armed forces. During the New Order, the police was part of the armed forces' command structure. Since 2000, the police have been responsible for security, order, law enforcement, and serving the public. Also, counterterrorism – an increasingly important task in Indonesia, especially since 2002 – is the responsibility of the police. The police have also been encouraged to improve their professional skills and knowledge. This separation led to new developments in police reform in Indonesia, including the involvement of international donors in police reform as well as the introduction of new philosophies of policing and notably community policing.[10] However, the police force remains a centralised organisation despite the decentralisation of government in the country.

The military's role includes defending the sovereignty and territorial integrity of the country and protecting the country from security threats. It also includes peacekeeping operations, civic missions, and assisting the police, based on demands regulated by the law. Certainly, the most important transformation of the role of the military in Indonesia is the ending of the dual function doctrine. The military was to become neutral in party politics, to withdraw from politics, and to respect democratic principles and human rights. The military relinquished its right for active service members to contest elected positions, such that, if members want to occupy a civilian position, they may now only do so after first retiring or resigning from the military. In addition, the ministry of defence has been led by a civilian since 1998, although most of the officials of the ministry are from the military, and the commander of the military is directly subordinate to the president, not the minister of the defence.

The Law on the Armed Forces of Indonesia, signed by President Megawati Sukarnoputri on 16 October 2004, mentions two basic duties for the military: namely (1) military operations for war and (2) military operations other than war. The fulfilment of these duties is to be based on the policy and political decisions of the state. It is interesting to note that the military operations other than war include the following roles and duties:

(1) Overcoming separatist movements;
(2) Overcoming armed rebellions against the legitimate government;
(3) Overcoming acts of terrorism;
(4) Securing the border areas;
(5) Securing vital and strategic national objects;
(6) Implementing world peace tasks in accordance with Indonesia's foreign policy;
(7) Protecting the president, vice president, and their families;
(8) Strengthening the capability of defence territories and their supporting forces;
(9) Helping local governments (in situations when the local government needs the facilities, equipment, and capabilities of the military to deal with disaster, rehabilitation, and communal conflicts);
(10) Helping the police to maintain security and order in accordance with the law;
(11) Helping with the protection of visiting heads of government and the representatives of foreign governments in Indonesia;
(12) Helping with the mitigation of natural disasters, displacement, and humanitarian assistance;

(13) Helping with search and rescue following accidents; and
(14) Helping the government with securing sealanes and airlines from hijacking, pirating, and smuggling.

Reformasi also brought change to the Attorney General's Office (AGO). The AGO had been dominated by military officers serving the interests of the Suharto regime, having served as "the judicial arms of the government through which the regime prosecuted, silenced, and punished its opponents, and protected its allies".[11] In addition, it functioned "no more than as the legal protector of the New Order regime and its supporters, especially the military. Cases that involved top military and government officials, for example, rarely went to a public court".[12] Since the Abdurrahman Wahid presidency, the AGO has become civilian in its organisation and has been dominated by civilian officials.[13] The AGO oversees the public prosecuting system, recruits and trains prosecutors, addresses public complaints, and provides legal advice to the government.

Despite reforms in the security sector in Indonesia, observers rightly indicate that there still remains a lot to be done. One of the challenges of SSR in Indonesia is how to strengthen the civilian oversight function of civil society and the parliament. Civil society organisations face challenges associated with the real and perceived "incompetence and inexperience of civilians in defence-related issues". [14] The oversight capacity of the parliament is another challenge. At present, the parliament possesses oversight tools that include committee hearings, hearings in plenary sitting, commissions of enquiry, parliamentary questions, the use of parliament question-time, interpellations, and referrals to the ombudsman. At least in formal terms, the Indonesian parliament has, following a period of significant democratisation, all the important oversight tools of a strong parliament. However, the role of the parliament in overseeing the military remains very limited.[15]

Although rarely studied, the role of the media in Indonesia is very important in strengthening civilian oversight by reflecting the opinions of citizens. The media, especially newspapers and television networks, are very active in their function in at least three important tasks of civilian oversight: first, the media reports citizens' complaints against the police and the military in Indonesia; second, the media monitors and reports irregularities and corruption in the police and the military; and third, the media informs the public and provides forums for debate on cases when the police fails to enforce the law. These multiple roles reflect the freedom of the press, the interest of citizens in SSR, and the presence of feedback mechanisms for the performance of the police and the military in Indonesia.

The Peace Process and SSR in Aceh

In many ways, the peace processes in Aceh conform to the common elements of war termination and peacemaking processes. C.R. Mitchell discusses these elements in his classic work on international conflict, which include "modification of coercive strategies, acceptance of some measure of failure or a need to compromise, and abandonment of at least some of the goals for which conflict behaviour was begun and costs and hardships borne".[16] As can be seen below, these elements are also crucial for improving governance and reform in the security sector in Aceh. Certainly, for both parties the peace process is complex, divisive, and long. In the light of subsequent developments, many of the measures taken and policies instituted with regard to these features suffered from setbacks and inconsistencies during the implementation phase.

Firstly, regime change in Jakarta facilitated a modification in the government's strategy toward the restive province. For more than two decades since the conflict erupted in 1976, the central government of Indonesia responded to the armed insurgency in Aceh with a counterinsurgency operation or "security approach". During the Suharto era, there was no negotiation between the central government and the rebel group. Indeed, the Indonesian military believed that the security approach was the only way to deal with the problem in Aceh. GAM, on the other hand, "adopted a military strategy of attrition and guerrilla warfare tactics, making use of its superior knowledge of the terrain and the population to counterbalance its lack of real military capacity".[17] There were no efforts from either side to explore alternative, nonviolent avenues to end the conflict.

It was not until the change of leadership in Jakarta in 1998 that any significant change in Jakarta's attitude toward the conflict in Aceh was clearly noticeable. In August 1998, President Habibie and the military Commander-in-Chief Wiranto visited the province, granted amnesty to hundreds of political prisoners, declared the end of a military operation known by its acronym DOM (*Daerah Operasi Militer* – military operation area), and made an unprecedented apology to the people of Aceh.[18] Habibie also introduced other new approaches to the problem in Aceh. The most important of these was the establishment of fact-finding missions to investigate human rights abuses in Aceh and the adoption of the new law on the Special Status of the Province of Aceh Special Region in 1999. This law, and the Law on Regional Government and Fiscal Balance between the Central Government and the Regions, both adopted in the same year, also increased the autonomous status of Aceh province.

These new approaches, however, took place in a very different context in Aceh. After the fall of Suharto, demands for independence in the province increased significantly. The wider context in which these demands were made was created by the fall of the authoritarian regime, the referendum for East Timor, and the taking place of general discussions on autonomy and federalism in Indonesia. Since February 1999, discourse on a referendum as a way to solve the problem of Aceh took centre stage. The idea spread among students in Aceh very rapidly, and they soon became the key proponents of the referendum agenda, visiting rural areas to 'socialise' among the population and promote the idea. Later, in September 1999 the *ulama*, Muslim legal scholars from traditional educational institutions in Aceh (*dayah*), announced their support for a referendum as the best way to deal with the problem in Aceh. Even the governor of Aceh and the provincial legislature supported the idea of a referendum: the governor stated that, for the people at the grassroots, a referendum means independence.[19]

The above conditions made peace negotiations impossible, as the language of the rebellion was increasingly framed in terms of self-determination, a norm enshrined in many international instruments including the Charter of the United Nations. This invited a harsher response from Jakarta and reinforced the commitment of the central government, especially that of the military, to frame its response in terms of the norm of territorial integrity, another well protected principle of international relations. The military launched several counterinsurgency operations that led to some of the worst human rights violations in the history of the conflict, including Idi Cut (3 February 1999), Simpang KKA (3 May 1999), and Bantaqiah (23 July 1999). GAM rebels terrorised and attacked the non-Acehnese population and their property in several districts, resulting in the displacement of thousands in Aceh and to North Sumatra, the nearby province. By the end of 1999, fear and insecurity had become common in daily life, as "local government had virtually ceased to operate in many areas along the north and east coasts".[20]

All of the conflict dynamics of the Habibie presidency continued into the Abdurrahman Wahid presidency (1999 – 2001) – military actions by both sides, accusations of human rights violations and attempted investigation of these violations, and policy controversies on the issues of a referendum and autonomy. The Wahid presidency, however, was marked with one crucial difference: for the first time in the history of the conflict, both sides agreed to attend mediation sessions in Switzerland, beginning in January 2000. With the assistance of the Henry Dunant Centre as a mediator, the Indonesian government and the rebel group reached an agreement in May 2000 known as the "Joint Understanding on Humanitarian Pause for Aceh". The agreement was only partially implemented, including elements such as the creation of a joint committee on security, a monitoring team, and some humanitarian action. The public in Aceh and the central government in Jakarta supported the agreement, but the military, the police, and many members of parliament, including the speaker, did not.[21] The agreement quickly collapsed.

Under President Megawati (2001-2004) another negotiation was attempted in February 2002, and an agreement, called "the Cessation of Hostilities Agreement" (CoHA), was finally reached on 9 December 2002. The agreement "called for the cantonment or storage of GAM weapons, the relocation and reformulation of the role of the Indonesian security forces, and the establishment of peace zones".[22] There was insufficient trust on both sides to support this agreement: GAM did not store its weapons in the 'placement sites', and the Indonesian military did not relocate. As a result, the agreement collapsed in April 2003.

However, significant changes occurred in the negotiation process that led to CoHA. GAM negotiators for the first time agreed to accept the autonomy law (called *Nanggroe Aceh Darussalam* – NAD Law) as a 'starting point' for discussion on the future of Aceh. The NAD Law was drafted during the Wahid presidency and entered into force in 2002. It presented the autonomy scheme as an alternative: a compromise between independence and integration. At the same time, GAM stressed its struggle for independence. The Government of Indonesia agreed to permit an international team of 'wise men' to participate in the negotiations.[23] The presence of the wise men reinforced the negotiation process and increased the involvement of the international community in the peace process. However, the efforts of the international community to renegotiate CoHA in Tokyo on 18 May 2003 failed, and the war resumed.

The Megawati government implemented increasingly harsh measures on 19 May 2003 in the form of a martial law that would last for a year. The government sent in more troops and police forces to the province. It was the largest military operation in the history of the conflict, and many rebels were killed in this new wave of violence. The military operation also limited the movement of the rebels, decreased their support base, and forced the rebels to resort to tactics such as extortion and hostage-taking for ransom.[24] Yet at the same time, a large-scale counterinsurgency operation, which increased the presence of military and police to 80,000 in Aceh, cost the government a large sum of money and offered no prospect of victory after a year. Admitting that the insurgents were not to be easily defeated, the commander of the Indonesian armed forces told the public "we cannot do what we hoped.... Two die but four take their place".[25]

In 2004, the new and democratically elected government, led by Susilo Bambang Yudhoyono and his vice president Jusuf Kalla, started a new peace process. While the previous peace processes in Aceh led to two cease-fire agreements (Humanitarian Pause and CoHA), the new peace process aimed at a comprehensive peace agreement. President Yudhoyono, himself a former general, told the nation that a political solution through negotiation was the only way to solve the problem in Aceh. Vice President Kalla, a successful and well-known businessperson, argued that war in Aceh was too expensive for the government to finance and that peace was much cheaper – an obvious conclusion. Determined to find a negotiated solution, both managed to convince the military, the political parties, and the parliament to support the peace process, which they started soon after coming to power in October 2004.[26] Martti Ahtisaari, former president of Finland, served as a mediator.

A combination of developments lies behind the historic deal that ended the conflict in Aceh. These include the election of a pro-peace president and vice president, sustained pre-negotiation preparation by Kalla and his trusted intermediaries, and the additional momentum towards a resolution created by the earthquake and tsunami of

December 2004. The most important development, however, was the drastic shift in the rebels' demands from independence to "self-government" within the state of Indonesia. This dramatic change took place in February 2005 during the second round of the five rounds of negotiation. The Government of Indonesia, on the other hand, agreed to a "self-government" solution for Aceh to replace the special autonomy status. Indonesia also agreed on the establishment of local political parties in Aceh. GAM's demand for local political parties was not new, but Indonesia had previously rejected the idea.[27]

During the fifth and final round of negotiations (12-17 July 2005), the GAM agreed that 3,000 fighters would stand down and that 840 weapons would be surrendered for destruction. These numbers were given to the mediation team on the last day of the negotiation. The mediation team then disclosed to the GAM that the Government of Indonesia had agreed that from 1 January 2006 only 14,700 soldiers would remain in Aceh, and the rest would be pulled out of the province. In addition, as many as 9,100 police officers would remain in Aceh. Apparently, the size of the police force was based on a police-citizen ratio of 1:400. However, the size of the military force was much higher than the 6,000 troops suggested in the previous rounds of negotiation.

The rule of law section of the MoU stated that the head of the Aceh administration would have power over the appointment of the chiefs of police and prosecutors serving in the province, and that civilian crimes committed by military personnel in Aceh would be tried in civil courts in Aceh. The MoU further stipulated that both a Human Rights Court and a Commission for Truth and Reconciliation would be established for Aceh, and that all participants in GAM activities would be granted amnesty within 15 days of the signing of the MoU.

The section on reintegration in the MoU committed the governments of Indonesia and Aceh to facilitating the reintegration into society of anyone who had participated in GAM activities, as well as civilians affected by conflict, through the establishment of a reintegration fund under the administration of the authorities of Aceh. It also affirmed the people's political, economic, and social rights, including the right to participate in political processes of all persons who had been granted amnesty or released from prison or detention; and the right of persons who had renounced their Indonesian citizenship during the conflict to regain it.

Peacebuilding and SSG in Aceh

The MoU immediately ended the war between the central government and the former combatants of GAM. According to the Multi-Stakeholder Review of Post-Conflict Programming in Aceh (MSR), "incidents between GAM and the government dropped to almost zero after the signing of the MoU in August 2005 and have remained low. Only five such incidents were reported between the start of 2006 and the end of 2008".[28]

However, to be durable in the implementation phase a peace agreement needs support from former adversaries as well as from wider stakeholders. In the case of Aceh, a UN peacekeeping operation was not possible, because Indonesia preferred regional organisations to be involved. A monitoring mission, mandated under security arrangements in the MoU, was then established consisting of elements from the former rebels, the Government of Indonesia, representatives of the Association of Southeast Asian Nations (ASEAN), and the European Union (EU). This mission, called the Aceh Monitoring Mission (AMM), lasted for one year and played an important role in overseeing the disarmament, demobilisation, and reintegration (DDR) programmes, as well as providing a framework for continuing cooperation among the parties and the wider community – both national and international – in dealing with post-agreement issues.

Both parties cooperated in the DDR processes, which was the first issue to be dealt with after the signing of the MoU. GAM demobilised all of its 3,000 combatants in accordance with the terms of the MoU. This number, however, was much smaller than the number of persons who were members of the military wing of GAM. In the implementation phase, there were 14,300 former GAM combatants in Aceh, less than 700 of whom (below 5 per cent) were women.[29]

In addition, the process of decommissioning all arms, ammunition, and explosives took place without incident. AMM assisted in this decommissioning process and played a key role in its success. Both the Indonesian military and former GAM combatants cooperated in the process. From September to December 2005, in four stages, the GAM submitted 840 weapons to be cut into pieces in ceremonies attended by former GAM members, the Indonesian security forces, representatives of the AMM, and the public. These weapons cutting ceremonies took place in different cities in Aceh. In December 2005, the military wing of the GAM was demobilised. The Aceh Transitional Committee (*Komite Peralihan Aceh* – KPA) was established as an organisation for former combatants with the purpose of reintegrating them into civilian life.[30]

In accordance with the MoU, amnesty was granted to GAM fighters detained by the Indonesian government. Immediately after the signing of the agreement and continuing until the end of August 2005, around 2,000 GAM members were granted amnesty. They, and former combatants who had gone into hiding in the hills, returned safely to their homes and were accepted by their communities – there were no instances of revenge violence and little tension with local communities, the military, the police, or the local government. In many cases, they were welcomed back as heroes. Their reintegration was also facilitated by several programmes of assistance for three groups, namely former combatants, political prisoners who received amnesty, and victims of conflict. These programmes included economic assistance, health care, and opportunities to participate in vocational trainings.[31]

Correspondingly, and in accordance with the MoU, the Government of Indonesia withdrew all elements of non-local military and police forces from Aceh, leaving local police forces responsible for upholding internal law and order in Aceh and, in normal peacetime circumstances, only local military forces present in Aceh to uphold external defence. The relocation of the security forces took place in four phases, from September to December 2005. By 31 December 2005, 31,681 security personnel (25,890 from the military and 5,791 from the police) were withdrawn from Aceh. The AMM supervised successful troop redeployment in the harbour of Lhokseumaue, North Aceh.[32]

After demobilisation and redeployment, the next challenge was to address some of the sources of hostility and, at the same time, to reinforce the peace in Aceh. In accordance with the MoU, the Law on the Governing of Aceh (LoGA) was enacted on 1 August 2006. LoGA was the result of post-MoU negotiations in Indonesia, involving the interests of many stakeholders. Some major breakthroughs were also provided for in the MoU, such as a clear definition of Aceh's special autonomy within the unitary Indonesian Republic, which was to be elucidated later in a new LoGA. The agreement and its implementation, therefore, provided an opportunity for participation in decision-making and policy-making, including in the area of security and development. The transformation of rebel groups into political parties was the most important development in the demilitarisation of politics in the post-conflict period in Aceh.

LoGA put most of the MoU into effect and made further provisions regarding government, security, local political parties, and other issues. The new law is based on the following principles: provincial and district government authority over all sectors of public affairs, excluding foreign affairs, external defence, national security, monetary and fiscal matters, justice, and freedom of religion; and a stipulation that all decisions on domestic or international affairs related to Aceh undertaken by the national government or legislature would be made in consultation with, and with the consent of, the legislature of Aceh and the head of the Aceh administration. This is a definition of "self government".

In addition, the MoU and LoGA allowed for the establishment and political participation of Aceh-based political parties, the right of the people of Aceh to nominate candidates for all elected offices, and the conduct of free and fair local elections within a specified timeline. After some delay, the first elections for the governorship of Aceh took place in December 2006. Candidates from or affiliated with GAM won the elections. At the district and city levels in 2007 and 2008, they succeeded in winning ten out of twenty-three districts and municipalities all over Aceh. In addition, former GAM members participated in the elections for local parliaments in the 2009 elections, winning either a plurality or a majority in the parliaments of the districts and municipalities where they had had a strong base of support during the rebellion. As mentioned earlier, in the 2012 elections, a former GAM leader and military commander won the elections for the governorship.

The nexus between security and development in Aceh can be seen from different angles. The MoU contains arrangements for issues such as the governance of Aceh, political participation, economic management, security, rule of law, dispute resolution, protection of human rights, the amnesty and reintegration of ex-combatants and political prisoners into society, and the establishment of the AMM. In other words, the MoU provides a framework to deal with some of the most important issues of security and development in post-conflict Aceh. With regard to one of the most contentious issues, the MoU stipulated that Aceh would retain 70 per cent of the revenue from all current and future hydrocarbon deposits and from other natural resources in the province and its territorial seas. Aceh would also enjoy direct and unhindered access to foreign countries, by sea and air. In addition to dealing with the status of natural resources as one of the most important issues, the economic section of the MoU provides a framework for the allocation of wealth to Aceh and, therefore, for increased access to resources for development in peacetime Aceh.

Besides the peace agreement, the Government of Indonesia plays an important role in peacebuilding, including DDR processes. This makes Aceh different from other cases where post-conflict peacebuilding has taken place in the context of a fragile or failed state, since Indonesia has, in contrast, a stable and democratic government with a growing economy. Therefore, the international donors and agencies that came to Aceh after the signing of the MoU in 2005, as well as the international organisations that changed their focus from tsunami relief to peacebuilding, were able to support the national, provincial, and district level governments in peacebuilding. One of the main challenges for the government and the donors was how to rebuild the economy in Aceh after the long war that caused such tremendous damage and expense.

At the time of writing, the peace has only been in place for seven years, and Aceh has only just crossed the so-called five-year threshold that marks the transition from a non-durable peace – when renewed war is most likely – to a more durable peace, when renewed war is less and less likely. The MoU has become the most durable peace deal made for Aceh. Peace in Aceh neutralised many of the threats to citizens originating from the state. It removed many forms of physical threats, such as abduction, torture, or execution; economic threats, such as damage to property and denial of access to work and resources; threats to rights, such as denial of basic civil liberties; and threats to position and status, such as public humiliation. It also removed threats to the security of citizens who came from the rebel groups, such as extortion, kidnapping for ransom, or revenge killings and harassment of people accused of cooperating with the Indonesian security forces.

Security Sector Actors in Aceh

The Military

Regarding defence and security matters, an important point agreed upon during the peace negotiations in Helsinki was the division of labour between the military and the police. After the agreement, soldiers in Aceh were no longer implicated to provide law and order. External defence would be a task only for the military, while keeping law and order would be a task solely for the police. This important point was not adopted in LoGA. Instead, Article 202 of LoGA states that the armed forces of Indonesia are responsible for the defence of the state and other tasks or duties in Aceh in accordance with the law. The defence of the state includes "to preserve, protect, and defend the integrity and sovereignty of the unitary state of the Republic of Indonesia, and other duties in accordance with the law, such as mitigating natural disasters, building transportation infrastructure, and other humanitarian duties after consultation with the Governor of Aceh."[33] The law also stipulates that the armed forces stationed in Aceh will uphold the universal principles of human rights and respect the traditions and customs of Aceh. It is apparent that the role of the military in LoGA is taken from the Law on the Armed Forces of Indonesia. Article 7 of this law mentions two basic duties of the military, namely (1) military operations for war and (2) military operations other than war. The fulfilment of these two duties should be based on the policy and political decisions of the state. In other words, from the perspective of a broader legal framework, the term "external defence" is too limiting and restricting, but, instead of amending the Law on the Armed Forces of Indonesia, LoGA adopted from it.[34]

Accordingly, the regional military command in Aceh in 2007 issued a strategic plan that included many elements of military operations other than war. These included the protection of strategic and vital national infrastructure; assisting the local government; assisting the police in maintaining law and order; dealing with armed separatist movements; overcoming armed rebellion, terrorism, and border security; and assisting in natural disaster management involving displaced people, as well as humanitarian assistance, implemented jointly with the local government and police. In Aceh, the most important "vital infrastructure" is the Exxon Mobil gas production compound in North Aceh. In 2006, as many as 1,200 security personnel were involved in protecting and securing this industrial site – 800 police; 350 army personnel; 28 marines; and 22 air force personnel. Exxon Mobil spent 1.8 billion rupiah per month for security. The number of security forces was slightly decreased in 2007, namely to a level of 1,000 personnel, of which 650 were from the police and 350 were from the military. Their roles included guarding the 141 km of pipeline and other vital installations.[35]

In 2006, further cooperation involving the police and the military took place during the elections. As many as 2,000 soldiers were deployed to assist the police, under the command of the regional police head. Originally, when the police requested the AMM for assistance in providing security during elections, the AMM suggested that former GAM members could be employed for security. The police, however, preferred to cooperate with the military and, with the agreement of the AMM, some 2,000 military officers were deployed during the elections. The involvement of the military in supporting the police to secure elections continued both in 2009 (for both the presidential and parliamentary elections) and in 2012 (for the governorship and district level elections).[36]

The new role of the military in Aceh constituted a marked improvement compared to the previous situation. During the civil war, the 'dual-function' of the military (which made the police part of the armed forces before 1999) enabled the military to play different roles in many aspects of citizens' lives, especially when Aceh was declared an area of military operation (*Daerah Operasi Militer* – DOM) and during counterinsurgency operations.[37] In addition, impunity characterised the military operations in Aceh. Peacebuilding limits the role the military can play – both in its military and non-military operation missions – to exceptional circumstances.

The Police

In the MoU and LoGA, the duty of the police is to maintain law and order. Although the GAM wanted the police in Aceh to be a decentralised authority, Article 204 of LoGA states that the police in Aceh are part of the centralised national police. LoGA also states that the police should coordinate with the governor regarding policies on tranquillity and order in Aceh, and that the police are responsible to the governor for the implementation of these policies. In their role as part of the national police force, the Aceh police are responsible to the national police head. Although not creating the Aceh police as a decentralised organisation, LoGA stipulates that the national police head of Indonesia needs written agreement from the governor in appointing the regional police head in Aceh. If the governor refuses to endorse the candidate for the regional police head, the national police head should nominate another candidate.

According to the MoU, the strength of the police in Aceh ought to be 9,100 officers. In reality, however, there are around 12,000 police officers in Aceh. One reason for this increase in number is that the national police college in Aceh continues to enrol new students. According to a police source, neither the governor nor the former GAM complained about this increase in the police force. The police in Aceh also protect the officials of the Reconstruction and Rehabilitation Agency as well as foreigners working in Aceh in the relief and humanitarian activities sector and, most recently, in post-conflict reconstruction and peacebuilding.

The Local Government Police

In Aceh, as well as in other parts of Indonesia, local governments at the provincial and district levels can establish a type of police unit that belongs to the local government, called *Satuan Polisi Pamong Praja* or Satpol PP. The task of this unit is to enforce regulations created by the local parliament. In Aceh, there is a special unit of this local police, called *Wilayatul Hisbah* (WH). Established by a governor's decree in 2004 and administered by the *Dinas Syariat Islam*, the WH is responsible for monitoring conduct and compliance to *Sharia* or Islamic bylaws within Acehnese society. This body does not have enforcement powers, but is authorised to provide 'moral guidance'. The national police, however, had to intervene to reestablish security when tension and social conflict emerged between Satpol PP and WH, on the one hand, and the community, on the other. The police in Aceh complained that, in addition to dealing with present security challenges in Aceh, such as illegal logging, armed robbery, as well as trafficking of illegal arms and drugs, they also need to deal with the spill-over policing problems created by the local government forces.[38]

Civil society organisations and human rights bodies in Aceh and beyond criticise both the Satpol PP and the WH. Satpol PP is criticised, firstly, for vigilantism, arbitrary arrest, and/or detention beyond their mandate and term of office and, secondly, for violating the rights of the urban poor, including street vendors and street children. WH is criticised for vigilantism based on Islamic bylaws, as implemented in Aceh – the only place in Indonesia that implements *Sharia* or Islamic bylaws. Cases of sexual harassment by WH officers have also occasionally emerged in the media and created outraged reactions both in Aceh and outside the province. Increasing oversight of these local government police forces is needed to enhance the security and well being of individuals and communities in Aceh.

The Aceh Transitional Committee and Former Combatants

Former combatants in Aceh constituted a disadvantaged group after the signing of the MoU. According to the "GAM Reintegration Needs Assessment",[39] their principle needs were primarily for livelihoods, housing, and health care. Younger ex-combatants wanted education and training as well. The Aceh Transitional Committee (*Komite Peralihan Aceh* – KPA) is an organisation established after the signing of the MoU to transform the military wing of the GAM into a civilian organisation. The leader of the KPA is the former commander of the GAM. During the first year of its establishment, the KPA played a crucial role in mobilising former GAM combatants to support the peace process, helping them to demobilise, and helping them reintegrate into civilian life.

The KPA, however, continues to maintain the hierarchical structures of the military wing of the GAM and, in some districts, tends to be separated from the larger community. This prolongs its conflict-era identity and hinders its members' full integration into society. In addition, reports indicate the involvement of some KPA members in extortion, intimidation, and other forms of crime.[40] Important elements of demobilisation were accomplished in Aceh within one year of the signing of the MoU. However, reintegration programmes for ex-combatants continue to be an important challenge to SSG in Aceh. According to the International Crisis Group, "in many areas, the KPA has become a thuggish, Mafia-like organisation that has created an atmosphere of fear"; and it may have become "the greatest scourge of post-conflict Aceh".[41]

The Militia

During the peace negotiations in Helsinki in 2005, there were concerns from the GAM about armed militia units in Aceh who worked for the Indonesian armed forces in their counterinsurgency operations. Their demand was for this militia to be formally disbanded and disarmed. The Government of Indonesia did not acknowledge the existence of the militia units and said that after the agreement the police would confiscate illegal arms from the public. Therefore, the issue of the militias did not appear anywhere in the MoU.

However, during the integration programmes after the MoU, the existence of the militias was acknowledged, including the Defenders of the Homeland (*Pembela Tanah Air* – PETA) and the Communication Forum for the Sons of the Nation (*Forum Komunikasi Anak Bangsa* – Forkab). As many as 6,500 members of militia units were included in the reintegration programme. They too received financial assistance and other reintegration benefits. Yet militia groups continued to constitute a threat to political stability and security in Aceh after the MoU.[42]

The Community and Civil Society

When the violence of the civil war and counterinsurgency operations ended and the peace agreement endured, most of the distortions in the security sector that directly affected the security of citizens also ended. Life then returned to normalcy, when individuals and communities were able to work, cooperate, and pursue their everyday interests and needs through non-coercive and nonviolent processes and exchanges in society. Farmers cultivated their lands, fishermen caught fish, parents took their kids to school, shop-owners opened their business until ten at night, and coffee houses opened for business until midnight. Peace, in other words, opened the way for a variety of micro-processes without or with very minimal intervention from the police, the justice system, and other centralised institutions and mechanisms. The role of the security sector is arguably the most significant part of the new state of security governance in Aceh that was facilitated by peacebuilding.[43]

An important survey, conducted in villages all over Aceh one year after the signing of the MoU, found that for villagers the security situation was extremely good. Therefore, for them, security and order was not a priority need as compared to road construction, livelihoods, job opportunities, education, or housing. Security and order was also found to be a lower priority issue as compared to healthcare and nutrition.[44] Only 10.9 per cent of villagers considered security and order a priority need in their village and among them only 2.2 per cent put security and order as the *first* priority. They needed information on the implementation of MoU, though, which was their top information priority. "Most Acehnese seem to see the success of the MoU as the most fundamental factor in their future prosperity and security".[45]

Local governance and institutions, which for a long period were hostage to civil war, began to resuscitate: for example, *Tuha Peut* or *Sorakopat*, a traditional village level governance body, returned to its role as a form of village level representative body, consisting of the *Keucik* (village head), *ulama* (local *Imam* or religious leader), knowledgeable village members, *adat* leaders,[46] farmers, and traders. The total number of members depends on the population of the village, although in Acehnese the term means 'four leaders'. The *Tuha Peut* provides advice and oversight in the area of customary law and religion for a village and manages disputes in these areas. Other traditional community organisations at the village level are farmers' groups (*Keujruen Blang*) and fishermen's groups (*Panglima Laot*). These traditional institutions are important for decision-making and dispute settlement at the lowest level of governance.[47]

Conclusion

In Indonesia, democratisation contributed to the peace process in Aceh, a province where a rebel group fought for independence for almost 30 years. Democratisation facilitated the introduction of new approaches that, while including elements of the previous approaches such as counterinsurgency, led to the initiation of the peace process. Two cease-fire agreements, one in 2000 and another in 2002, and a peace agreement, or MoU, were the outcomes of the peace process. Furthermore, the democratic institutions of the country have sustained the durability of the peace agreement in Aceh since 2005. These include a system of decentralised government or regional autonomy, a competitive electoral and party system, and the decreasing role of the military in politics and conflict management.

When the popularly elected president and leaders of the rebel group in Aceh decided to go to the negotiation table, the larger environment of democratisation enabled them to sustain the peace process and the peacebuilding efforts that followed.

The peace process in Aceh significantly transformed SSG. The MoU stopped the killings, paving the way for the implementation of the DDR process, and established freedom of movement for the citizenry. Security actors, both of the statutory and non-statutory kinds, as well as civil society actors now function within a normal, peaceful, and democratic environment. Democratic oversight remains weak, but peace and democracy in Indonesia in general and in Aceh specifically will not inhibit the emergence of enhanced oversight in the future. In fact, many objectives of oversight can be reached through other means. To the extent that, due to democratisation, the military is no longer a superior organisation, and the military and the police are no longer geared toward counterinsurgency operations, it follows that vital objectives of oversight in Aceh and elsewhere in Indonesia have been realised. Finally, to the extent that leaders are competing through political parties and democratic elections, and that the civilian leadership controls the security forces, then other important objectives of oversight may also be fulfilled.

Certainly, the results of democratisation and the peace process in Aceh are not flawless. Former combatants established local political parties, participated in elections, and aimed at winning the elections. However, they used violence and intimidation in the process of winning elections. In the 2012 elections, Irwandi Yusuf accused the Aceh Party of using intimidation and violence, while in 2006 the losing candidates had accused Yusuf and his running mates of the same crimes. The police are no longer part of the armed forces, and members of the police attend workshops on human rights standards or community policing, as they try to change their image and win the trust of citizens. Nevertheless, the police remain one of the most corrupt institutions. Their capacity to enforce the law and investigate violence related to elections in Aceh remains underdeveloped.

In other words, the outcomes of democratisation and the peace process are mixed and unstable. Therefore, in the words of Timothy Sisk, we must have "sober expectations about the partial and restricted nature of outcomes in post-war transitions: neither the peace-making nor the democratisation aims are likely to be fully realised in the transitional process".[48] In this situation, it is very important to think about ways in which the accomplishment of reform in Aceh may endure and become stronger.

Notes

1 *The Jakarta Post*, 5 May 2012, p. 2.

2 R.M. Goldman, *From Warfare to Party Politics: The Critical Transition to Civilian Control* (New York: Syracuse University Press, 1990), pp. 9-10.

3 A.K. Jarstad and T.D. Sisk (eds.), *From War to Democracy: Dilemmas of Peacebuilding* (New York: Cambridge University Press, 2008), pp. 17-36.

4 S. Clark and B. Palmer, *Peaceful Pilkada, Dubious Democracy: Aceh's Post-Conflict Elections and their Implications* (Jakarta: The World Bank, 2008), pp. iii- 4.

5 A.K. Jarstad, "Dilemmas of War-to-Democracy Transitions: Theories and Concepts" in Jarstad and Sisk (eds.), *From War do Democracy*, p. 17.

6 *Security Sector Governance and Reform*, DCAF Backgrounder 05/2009 (Geneva: Geneva Centre for the Democratic Control of Armed Forces, 2009), p. 1.

7 Harold Crouch, *Political Reform in Indonesia after Soeharto* (Singapore: ISEAS, 2010), p. 7.

8 *Ibid*, p. 133.

9 *Ibid*, p. 144; J. Pramodhawardhani and Mufti Makaarim, *Reformasi Tentara Nasional Indonesia* (Jakarta: IDSPS & DCAF, 2009); and B.W. Umar, *Reformasi Kepolisian Republik Indonesia* (Jakarta: IDSPS & DCAF, 2009).

10 E. Lachica, *Examining the Role of Foreign Assistance in Security Sector Reforms: The Indonesian Case* (Singapore: IDSS, 2003).

11 R. Sukma and E. Prasetyono, *Security Sector Reform in Indonesia: The Military and the Police* (The Hague: Clingendael, 2003), p. 16.

12 *Ibid.*

13 *Ibid.*

14 *Ibid.*, p. 29.

15 E. Schneier, "Evolving Patterns of Legislative Oversight in Indonesia", in R. Stapenhurst et.al (eds.), *Legislative Oversight and Budgeting: A World Perspective* (Washington, D.C.: The World Bank, 2008), pp. 201-215.

16 C.R. Mitchell, *The Structure of International Conflict* (London: Macmillan, 1981), p. 166.

17 K.E. Schulze, "From the Battlefield to the Negotiating Table: GAM and the Indonesian Government 1999-2005", *Asian Security*, vol. 3, no. 2, 2007, p. 84.

18 Crouch 2010, p. 285; M.A. Miller, *Rebellion and Reform in Indonesia: Jakarta's Security and Autonomy Policies in Aceh* (New York: Routledge, 2009), p. 21 and 27.

19 E. Aspinall and H. Crouch, *The Aceh Peace Process: Why it Failed* (Washington, D.C.: East-West Center, 2003), pp. 7-8.

20 Crouch 2010, p. 286.

21 M.A. Miller, *Rebellion and Reform in Indonesia: Jakarta's Security and Autonomy Policies in Aceh* (New York: Routledge, 2009), pp. 79-80.

22 Schulze 2007, pp. 90-91.

23 Aspinall and Crouch 2003, p. 27; and Schulze 2007, p. 90.

24 Schulze 2004, pp. 28-29.

25 E. Aspinall, *The Helsinki Agreement: A more promising basis for peace in Aceh?* (Washington, D.C.: East West Center, 2005), p. 12.

26 M. Morfit, "The Road to Helsinki: The Aceh Agreement and Indonesia's Democratic Development", *International Negotiation*, vol. 12, 2006, pp. 111-143.

27 Miller 2009, p. 158.

28 MSR, *Multi-Stakeholder Review of Post-Conflict Programming in Aceh: Identifying the Foundations for Sustainable Peace and Development in Aceh* (December 2009), p. 97.

29 *Ibid.*, p. 18.

30 Miller 2009, p. 161.

31 MSR 2009, pp. 56-60.

32 Miller 2009, p. 161.

33 Law on the Governing of Aceh, article 208.

34 Law on the Armed Forces of Indonesia, article 7.

35 S. Yanuarti, "Pergeseran Peran TNI Pasca MoU Helsinki" in Ikrar Nusa Bhakti (ed.), *Beranda Perdamaian: Aceh Tiga Tahun Pasca MoU Helsinki* (Yogyakarta: Pustaka Pelajar & P2P LIPI, 2008), p. 247.

36 *Ibid.*, p. 242.

37 I.K. Bhakti, *Reformasi Sektor Keamanan: Sebuah Pengantar* (Jakarta: IDSPS & DCAF, 2009), pp. 4-5.

38 S.N. Siregar, "POLRI dan Pengelolaan Keamanan Pasca MoU Helsinki" in Bhakti (ed.), p. 276.

39 World Bank, *GAM Reintegration Needs Assessment: Enhancing Peace through Community-Level Development Programming* (Jakarta: The World Bank, 2006).

40 MSR, 2009.

41 International Crisis Group (ICG), "GAM vs GAM in the Aceh Elections", *Asia Briefings*, 123 (Jakarta/Brussels, 2011), p. 7.

42 MSR 2009, p. 126.

43 K. Clements, "Toward a Sociology of Security" *Conflict Research Consortium*, Working Paper 90, July 1990.

44 World Bank, *2006 Village Survey in Aceh: An Assessment of Village Infrastructure and Social Conditions the Kecamatan Development Program* (Jakarta: The World Bank, 2007), p. 67.

45 *Ibid.*, p. 88.

46 Adat leaders are traditional leaders, custodians of custom and customary law.

47 *Ibid.*, p. 76; and MSR 2009, p. 143, and p. 155.

48 T. Sisk, "Peacebuilding as Democratization: Findings and Recommendations" in Jarstad and Sisk (eds.), *From War to Democracy*, p. 240.

2 *Peacebuilding and Security Sector Governance in the Philippines*

CAROLINA G. HERNANDEZ

Since the last decades of the twentieth century, the world has seen an increasing number of internal conflicts where the protagonists are from inside the nation state. Among the most important causes of this phenomenon is the rise of multi-ethnic and highly diversified societies upon which the post-independence nation state was built. Asia has been an arena where this phenomenon continues to challenge contemporary governments and societies. Whether in South or Southeast Asia, conflict-riven societies have witnessed the horrendous human and material consequences of internal violence. In each of these cases, whether it is communist insurgency or ethnic separatism, a main party to the conflict is the government.

The late twentieth century saw the phenomenal rise of new democracies (often referred to as "third wave" democracies)[1] out of authoritarian regimes, followed by an important body of academic literature, arguing that a critical element of democratisation is the institutionalisation of democratic control of armed forces.[2] Subsequent thinking focussed on democratisation and improving governance to deliver both security and development to peoples by making democratising governments more effective and responsive to the needs of their citizens. This led to the realisation that the democratic control of armed forces – usually preceded by institutional and functional separation of the police from the military – is a necessary but not sufficient requirement for good democratic governance. Moreover, adopting a broader view of the critical actors in the promotion and achievement of good democratic governance became necessary in order to bring about both security and development[3] in societies, whether under conditions of violence or periods of peace. This realisation involved both the academic (or epistemic) and policy communities whose parallel efforts led to the contemporary understanding of security sector governance (SSG), security sector reform (SSR), peacebuilding, security, and development, as well as their links to each other.

This chapter seeks to explore the issue of peacebuilding, SSG and SSR in the Philippines with some emphasis on the situation in the conflict-affected areas in Mindanao as relevant. It examines the Philippine case in the context of the relationship between SSG and SSR on the one hand and peacebuilding on the other, as well as how SSG affects the provision of security and development to the public. It then analyses the role and performance record of security actors and oversight institutions in the Philippines, before examining the outstanding challenges facing the country in this regard. It concludes with a brief discussion of future prospects.

SSG and Peacebuilding

Defining SSG/SSR requires a definition of 'security' and the 'security sector'. Leaving the definition of security aside for a moment, definitions of the security sector have taken at least three approaches: minimalist, middle-ground, and maximalist. The minimalist definition of the security sector limits its scope to the uniformed (police, military, and paramilitary) and intelligence services, the judiciary, and border and customs officials.[4] A middle-range approach defines the sector to include the statutory security forces or uniformed services, security management and oversight bodies, justice and enforcement institutions, and non-statutory security forces; or put alternatively, the organisations authorised to use force, civil management and oversight bodies, justice and law enforcement institutions, non-statutory security forces and non-statutory civil society groups.[5] A maximalist approach includes in the security sector statutory security forces (armed forces, paramilitary forces, intelligence and secret services, police, border and customs officials, reserve units); non-statutory security forces (private militia, private security companies, private military organizations, liberation armies, guerrilla armies, organised crime groups, nationalist terrorist movements); and instances of civilian management, such as the executive (including a national security council, ministries of defence, internal affairs, and foreign affairs, financial management bodies), the legislature (parliament, parliamentary committees, commissions), elements of the judiciary and wider legal framework (constitutional framework, judiciary, Ministry of Justice, prison regime, Human Rights Commission, Ombudsman), and civil society (NGOs, media, think-tanks, research institutes, public opinion-makers, the electorate, political parties, and the business community).[6] This chapter will adopt a middle ground approach not only for manageability, but also due to the fact that it will draw heavily from an ongoing study by the Institute for Strategic and Development Studies (ISDS) that uses this approach, namely the development of a Security Sector Reform Index (SSRI).[7]

The term 'security', on the other hand, has acquired a meaning beyond the earlier state-centric focus on the military and defence capabilities for warding off external military aggression.[8] Since the end of the Cold War, human security – based on the individual's freedom from fear and freedom from want – has achieved wide acceptance;[9] and, although still state-centric, comprehensive security includes different, though interconnected, dimensions (military, political, economic, cultural, ecological, etc.).[10] While still conceptually problematic, human security is increasingly being used by advocates of SSR/SSG in the academic and policy communities, if only to highlight the relevance of 'freedom from fear' to the function of security provision by the security sector. Moreover, an expansion of the meaning of security continues to face resistance in societies, which appropriately oppose the role expansion of statutory security forces in society.[11] Thus, the physical security, or 'freedom from fear', aspect of human security is unlikely to find easier acceptance in these societies than its 'freedom from want' component, due to the misperceived implications of an expanded role for statutory security forces in the governance of society at large.

SSR is said to have emerged after the end of the Cold War when it framed the transitions of countries in Eastern and Central Europe. There, authoritarian governments with military partners became democratic governments, whose armed forces were brought under civilian control. From its post-Cold War origins in Europe, the idea of SSR spread to other countries undergoing political transition, as well as societies going through domestic conflict and post-conflict transitions. SSR contexts may now include political transitions from authoritarianism to democracy, conflict and post-conflict situations, as well as developed democracies, which also need "to optimise the management, efficiency and accountability of their security sectors".[12]

In the case of the Philippines, the national level context of SSG and SSR is political transition, but the local level contexts in conflict-affected areas in Mindanao, for example, reflect features of both conflict and post-conflict settings within the broader national context of political transition. One cannot deal adequately with SSG and SSR issues in Mindanao without taking the national level context into account, particularly because the Philippines is a unitary state with strictly defined powers between the central and local governments. The 1991 Local Government Code[13] devolved substantive powers to the local government units, but not the power of civilian oversight over the armed forces.

Security and Development

There is an inextricable link between security and development. A multi-disciplinary, multi national and multi-year study conducted by the ISDS established links between security and development broadly defined, demonstrating that security and development were two faces of the same coin of human well-being,[14] as hypothesised by an earlier project.[15] Through the lenses of comprehensive and human security, the probable links between security, development, democracy, governance and civil-military relations in an increasingly interdependent world were explored, and these links were validated within the context of Southeast Asia from a conceptual point of view and with substantive empirical referents.

It is easy to understand that without good governance of the security sector, the comprehensive security of the government and the human security of its citizens are unachievable; and that without peace over a reasonably long period of time, development for both the individual and society across many dimensions (economic, social, material, physical, ecological, etc.) is similarly unachievable. Despite its weaknesses and the enormous challenges – especially those wrought by the unprecedented expansion of human capacities, which the technological revolution facilitated – it is within a democratic polity that human empowerment and human equality can best be served. In a democratic setting, the political spaces for accountability, transparency, responsiveness, responsibility, and participation in governance are better assured. Therefore, good SSG requires a functioning democracy.

In the Philippines, comprehensive security for the government and human security for its citizens has remained elusive despite the restoration of democracy in 1986. Although political succession through elections[16] is usually respected, there have been two instances of extra constitutionally-based succession – from Ferdinand Marcos to Cory Aquino in February 1986, and from Joseph Estrada to Gloria Macapagal-Arroyo in January 2001 – in which the uniformed services unfortunately played a critical role. This is the reason why, with the consistent decline in the popularity of Macapagal-Arroyo and her government's inability to accommodate the family and personal interests of key political and economic actors in Philippine politics, a coalition sought to destabilise the Macapagal-Arroyo administration in 2006[17], bringing together civilians with the uniformed services – particularly the Philippine Marines (PM) and the First Scout Ranger Regiment (FSSR) of the Philippine Army, whose military units have been at the forefront of the counter-operations against the communist insurgency and ethnic separatism since the 1970s.

Since the imposition of martial law in 1972, the military and the police have also played a key role in regime survival and maintenance. In the seven coup attempts against the government of Cory Aquino during 1986-1989, the 'constitutionalist' elements of the uniformed services fought a number of military units that sought to depose Aquino and thereby ensured the survival of her government.[18] Similarly, the goal of deposing Macapagal-Arroyo through the Oakwood Mutiny of July 2003, Operation Hackle of February 2006, and the associated Manila Peninsula Incident, was frustrated by the chain of command of the Armed Forces of the Philippines (AFP) who remained loyal to the constitution.

At the national level, although constitutional and legal measures had been adopted to democratise civil-military relations, including the primacy of the principle of the supremacy of civilian authority over the military at all times and the institutional and functional separation of the police from the military, the task of consolidating democracy remained an elusive goal. Military influence and participation in politics continued to characterise civil-military relations in the country, a situation that impacts on the delivery of security and development to the population, especially in conflict areas, including Mindanao.[19]

The probable relationship between peace, human security, and human development was explored by the 2005 Philippine Human Development Report, which focused on this theme. Adopting a broader definition of human security by going beyond 'freedom from fear' and 'freedom from want', the report included 'freedom from humiliation'.[20] Among its findings the report noted the inexorable links between peace, human security, and human development, in which conflict, or the absence of peace, constituted a critical constraint not only to human security, but also to several indices of human development. Among the 22 provinces in the Philippines with the highest number of armed encounters between 1986 and 2004, 15 were located in Mindanao.[21] According to the report, these conflict-prone areas were among the country's lowest ranked provinces in terms of human development performance, showing the likely link between lack of security and low human development.[22] The human costs of conflict in Mindanao also showed a total of 60,000 dead, 54,000 wounded, and 350,000 displaced between 1969 and 1996[23], demonstrating thereby the deadly implications of armed conflict for the physical security of peoples.

The foregoing observations are indicative of the importance of peace to both security and development in the Philippine case. The quality of SSG in the conflict areas is also an important element in peacebuilding, as illustrated in two cases studied by ISDS in the context of its ongoing SSRI project. These cases both took place in communist insurgency prone areas in the Visayas, and not under conditions of ethnic separatism as found in Mindanao. Nevertheless, they are instructive as to how good SSG among key security sector actors from the uniformed services, the local government, and civil society can make a difference in the building of peace, and conversely, how the persistence of conflict might be abated by good SSG.

These cases are Bohol Province and the municipality of Leon in Iloilo Province in the Visayas, Central Philippines.[24] Both cases can be considered 'success' stories and best practices for SSG. Bohol Province moved rapidly from being among the poorest Philippine provinces to a rapidly growing, peaceful, and politically stable province. It has since been developing rapidly and marketing itself as among the newest tourist destinations in the country, learning at the same time from the negative ecological and cultural effects of run-away tourism in other places. In Iloilo Province, functional and institutional cooperation, whereby key actors operated within their areas of responsibility and observed the norms of accountability and transparency, moderated conflict in the municipality of Leon, despite the continuing influence of the Communist Party of the Philippines' New People's Army (CPP-NPA) in many villages.[25]

Security Providers in the Philippines

It must be stated from the outset that the term 'security providers' is highly contested. Within the SSR/SSG epistemic community, this term refers to those groups, agencies and individuals that assume the task of providing physical security to the people. They are either statutory (i.e., authorised by the laws of the state), or non-statutory (i.e., self-appointed or organised groups that seek to provide an alternative to legally authorised agencies and officials, and thus may include rebel and organised criminal groups and private military security corporations). The fact that many 'security providers' have not only failed to provide physical security, but have caused their insecurity is well known and recognised as a global reality. This has contributed to poor SSG in many parts of the world and validates the need for SSR.

Statutory Security Actors

The main statutory security actors in the Philippines are the military and the police, charged with the constitutional and legal duty to provide for external defence against foreign aggression, internal security against domestic insurgency and separatism, as well as peace and order. The Citizens Armed Forces Geographical Units (CAFGU) are the current version of the village self-defence units used against the so-called Huks insurgents or Liberation Army against Japan (*Hukbong Magpapalaya Laban sa Hapon*) in the 1950s. Organised, armed, and controlled by the AFP, the CAFGU's legal mandate is to fight insurgents alongside the military and the police in conflict areas.

Philippine colonial ties to the United States (US) inhibited the development of an external security role for the AFP.[26] From the beginning of the military's establishment, following the adoption of Commonwealth Act No. 1 or the National Defense Act of 1935, the role of the Philippine military has been to provide for internal defence and peace and order. This resulted from the fact that external defence had been assumed by the US since the period of American colonisation in 1896[27], and the subsequent reconstitution of the Philippine Constabulary (PC) – the country's national police force in charge of peace and order – as part of the Philippine military. When the Philippines acquired formal independence from the US in 1946, the military's responsibility for internal defence and peace and order did not change as the military alliance with the US ensured that external defence would continue to be provided by Washington. Subsequent military assistance and bases agreements with the US cemented this division of labour in security provision between the military organisations of the two countries. Thus, until the present, the AFP's external defence capability remained inadequate while its continued internal defence function resulted in the enhancement of the military's ability to move, to shoot, and to communicate – capabilities suited for counterinsurgency rather than for war against an external enemy.[28]

It is this inadequate capacity of the AFP that must have led the Philippine government to re-engage the US as an ally, a condition facilitated by the attacks on the World Trade Center in New York City on 11 September 2001 (9/11). US perceptions that Southeast Asia had become the 'second front' in the global war against terrorism[29] added to the Philippines' strategic weight and softened negative US attitudes towards Manila following the withdrawal of its basing rights in the Philippines. This also facilitated the resumption of joint military exercises between the two countries: the *Balikatan* exercises, for example, are seen as an opportunity to improve Philippine military capacity, as well as interoperability between the two armies. Attendant to the *Balikatan* exercises was the Visiting Forces Agreement (VFA) which defined the status of US forces in the Philippines and was typical of similar agreements with other US allies in the region and beyond. Another important agreement that is seen as contributing to the improvement of Philippine military capacity is the Mutual Logistics and Support Agreement, which enables the Philippine military to access war material and equipment no longer needed by the US military once exercises and military assistance activities in the Philippines had been concluded. This excess war material and equipment are in effect transferred to the AFP without any financial obligation.

The second most important statutory security actor in the country is the Philippine National Police (PNP). Its history has been conjoined with that of the Philippine military since the planned ten-year period of self-rule (1935-1945) under the Philippine Commonwealth that was meant to precede formal independence. However, when World War II cut short this ten-year period, the Philippines was abruptly plunged into independence soon after the end of the war. The history of the PC (constabulary) and the PNP (police) is linked to the multidimensional challenges of the post-war period and related to the country's internal security.

Domestic conflict has marked the Philippine political landscape almost since the moment of its independence from the US in 1946. An agrarian-based communist insurgency, with an ideological model inspired by the former Soviet Union, flared up soon after the first post-independence elections. Elected members of the Socialist Party of the Philippines were denied the seats they won during the elections because of the fear that they would not support the adoption of the Parity Amendment to the 1935 Philippine Constitution. This amendment granted equal rights to US citizens to exploit the country's natural resources. At the same time, the legitimacy of the former guerrilla group – the Huks – that had fought on the side of the US against Japan during the war was not recognised and they were thus not entitled to veterans benefits from the US.

The Huks operated in Central Luzon and parts of the Visayas, where over time absentee landlordism became institutionalised.[30] The PC, as a national police force, could not avail itself of the same type of military assistance that had been extended to the Philippine military under the bilateral military assistance agreement with the US. The Philippine government decided to merge the PC with the Philippine military in order for the PC to gain access to US military assistance.[31] Over time, there developed some form of 'incestuous' relationship between the PC and the military where the PC would be integrated with the military, or separated from it, as dictated by the 'national security' considerations of the day. For example, the police forces that used to be under the administrative control and supervision of local chief executives (i.e. city and municipal mayors and provincial governors) were affected when 'national security', interpreted as 'Marcos regime security', required the centralisation of all the country's uniformed services.

In 1975 in an effort to establish centralised control over the country's uniformed services (i.e. the AFP, the PC, and local police forces), Marcos decreed the integration of all police forces in the country with the PC. Thus, the PC became the fourth major service command of the AFP (together with the army, air force, and navy). The Integrated National Police (INP) was put under the PC, an arrangement in which there was only one head for both organisations. This put the PC-INP, for all intents and purposes, together with the AFP leadership, under the President as Commander-in Chief of the AFP. Thus, all the statutory security actors were put under the direct control of President Marcos. This unusual arrangement came to an end shortly after 1986 with the extra-constitutional end of authoritarian rule under Marcos and the restoration of a democratic regime under Cory Aquino.

The legal separation of the police from the military was achieved through the enactment of Republic Act No. 6975 (RA 6975, otherwise known as the PNP Law) in 1991 pursuant to the relevant provisions of the new 1987 constitution. The PNP was established and put under the administrative supervision and control of a newly organised Department of the Interior and Local Government. No longer under the authority of the local chief-executives, control of the police forces was in theory centralised under the remit of a civilian government agency. In practice, however, local chief-executives exercise a degree of administrative control over the police forces assigned to their locality. Under the law, in addition to the provision of peace and order, the police were to be in charge of internal security. However, the resurgence of the communist insurgency under the CPP-NPA, as well as the persistence of Muslim separatism, led to the enactment of a new law in 1998 – Republic Act No. 8551 – returning the internal security function to the AFP. The AFP became the principal internal security provider while the PNP was made to play a supporting role in counterinsurgency in addition to its core function of peace and order.

The CAFGU, on the other hand, is the current version of an earlier village-based self-defence unit used in the counterinsurgency against the Huks during the 1950s. Like its predecessor, the CAFGU are supposed to be under the control of the AFP, but in many instances are used by politicians, local leaders, or businesses for their private purposes. They are generally poorly trained and ill-equipped, often likely perpetrators of human rights violations, and receive a meagre salary. The CAFGU were organised through an executive order issued by Cory Aquino in 1987.[32] The current size of the CAFGU is estimated to be about 46,827, organised into 741 CAFGU companies within the Philippine Army.

Despite the presence of an adequate constitutional and legal framework defining the structures and functions of these statutory security actors, they have not been able to discharge their security provision functions properly and consistently.[33] For instance, over time the military and the police developed notoriety for extracting 'rents' from local communities, particularly in remote areas. Threats of physical harm compel people to comply with these rent-seeking demands. Physical torture of suspected rebels and ordinary criminals by the military and the police is also well known. In fact, their human rights record, especially during the authoritarian period of the Marcos presidency, is dismal: they have been cited by various human rights groups for physical torture and the extra-judicial killing of suspects under their custody.[34]

Non-statutory Security Actors

There are several non-statutory security actors in the Philippines at present. Among them are the CPP-NPA,[35] the Bangsa Moro Islamic Armed Forces (BIAF), which is the armed component of the Moro Islamic Liberation Front (MILF),[36] the Abu Sayyaf Group (ASG), the Moro National Liberation Front (MNLF – a breakaway group loyal to Nur Misuari), and the private armies of politicians and transnational crime groups. Furthermore, there is a host of private security companies that provide security guards to private establishments, including banks, hotels, and shopping malls, as well as private homes, individually or collectively, in gated residential areas. Also, there are a few foreign private military and security corporations (PMSCs) that recruit military and police personnel and/or are engaged in security operations in the country.[37] PMSCs operating in the country usually provide security to businesses in the extractive industry sector, such as mining.

The longest-running communist insurgency in the region is found in the Philippines.[38] Peace talks with the CPP-NPA-NDF (National Democratic Front, the CPP's alleged front organisation) have failed despite mediation by third parties, including by Norway.[39] The NPA is reputed to provide 'security and justice' to villages it either controls or influences, and accounts of its 'security' provision to these villages, including speedy or instant 'administration of justice' to perpetrators of social injustice and oppression, abound. At the same time, it is able to extract taxes from the businesses that operate in these areas: these include protection moneys paid to the NPA by transportation and communication companies. Failure to comply leads to the burning of buses, or bombing of cell sites of mobile phone service providers.[40] During elections, the NPA also exacts 'permit to campaign' fees from politicians who are even issued receipts for theses fees either in cash or in kind, the latter usually involving firearms.[41]

The BIAF provides 'security' to conflict areas in Mindanao, particularly where conflict arises between the MILF and government forces. Heir to the Muslim separatist movement, the MILF was established in 1978 and was originally confined to the Maguindanao faction of the MNLF. Now it has members from other ethnic groups that follow the religion of Islam. In the beginning of the year 2000, it had some 15,000 armed fighters and constituted the largest non-statutory security actor in the country at that time. By late 2005, the MILF exercised varying degrees of influence in 1,463 out of 6,909 villages in the three regions in Mindanao involved in ethnic separatism.[42] The MILF is seen as "Southeast Asia's most formidable armed separatist organisation, with 10,000 to 15,000 men under arms at any time, and tens of thousands more part-time reservists on call".[43] This rise to pre-eminence is associated with "the immersion of foreign terrorists in the Mindanao insurgency and with the splintering of the MNLF".[44] Presumably, it is able to provide 'security' to the population residing in these villages.

The MILF-BIAF can be augmented at any time by armed civilians, who can be called upon to join in the fight against government forces. One call to which Muslims outside of the BIAF would join in the fight against the government would be a call to *jihad*, as was issued by the movement's late leader Hashim Salamat. The MILF is also suspected of using child soldiers as recruits.[45] This call to arms is probably a factor in the alleged links between the MILF-BIAF and the ASG, a basically kidnap-for-ransom gang whose origins go back to ex-MNLF militants who formed their own group in 1991 under the late Abdulrajak Janjalani and operated on Basilan Island, and in Zamboanga City and Sulu in Mindanao.[46] The ASG has 200-500 members at any one time.[47] The fruits of the ASG's criminal activities are believed to benefit the families and clans of its members who also are provided physical and economic security by the gang members.

Although the MNLF under Nur Misuari concluded a peace agreement with the Philippine government during the tenure of former President Fidel Ramos in 1996, when Misuari was removed as governor of the Autonomous Region for Muslim Mindanao (ARMM), some 200 of his supporters rose up in protest against the government. He was subsequently placed under house arrest by the government, while his followers in the MNLF went underground. Since then, this breakaway wing of the MNLF has operated as an insurgent-secessionist group, much like the MILF.[48]

As part of the peace agreement with the MNLF, the government integrated some 7,000 out of the estimated 17,700 MNLF fighters into the AFP and the PNP. Integration took place without the usual prior demilitarisation and demobilisation phases of disarmament, demobilisation and reintegration (DDR) of former combatants. Unfortunately, not all of those who were integrated were actual MNLF fighters, but were instead their nominees, or so-called 'successors'. Those who were not integrated either turned to farming, joined the MILF, the Misuari Breakaway faction, or formed their own 'lost command' groups, kidnap-for-ransom gangs or terrorist groups.[49] On the whole, the integration programme following the peace accord with the MNLF fell short of the usual goals of DDR in post-conflict situations.[50]

A long-standing practice, although also long outlawed in the Philippines, is the use of private armies by politicians, transnational criminal groups, and even some churches. In the past, Filipinos believed that winning in Philippine elections required 'guns, goons, and gold'. It is obvious that these three factors of election success are inter-related since one cannot afford to buy arms or have goons work for a candidate without the possession of gold. Private armies served as the guns and goons of powerful political clans whose 'persuasive' tactics and practices were used to deliver votes for their principals. At present, private armies are also used by transnational criminal groups and some churches. There were reportedly some 91 private armies operating in the Philippines in 2007.[51] When martial law was imposed in the Philippines in 1972, rumours circulated that the attempt by the military and the police to enter the headquarters of a powerful church group was repulsed by the latter's private army, which curiously and anomalously allegedly included members of the military and the police. This same church group's private army allegedly refused to allow the current president to bring in his security group when he called on the church leadership to thank them for their support in the presidential election in May 2010. Such practices represent a challenge to state authority and could further undermine the presently poor state of SSG

Private security companies operating in the Philippines have grown exponentially over the past few decades. They are known to have been established for profit by retired military and police officers, or by members of powerful political families. They provide protection for private businesses, private homes, and gated communities, as well as schools and universities. Often called 'blue guards' after the colour of their uniforms, they are often low-paid and are not in the company's roster of regular employees. Consequently, they do not enjoy social security and other benefits enjoyed by regular employees. Some of their members have allegedly been involved in a number of crimes, such as robbery, blackmail operations, and identity theft.

Finally, there are apparently some instances where foreign PMSCs operate in the Philippines. They reportedly recruit active duty and retired military and police personnel for foreign operations. The US-based PMSC Academi (formerly Blackwater) is known to have recruited and deployed these types of recruits in Iraq and Afghanistan. To what extent this practice is found in the Philippines, as well as whether and how foreign recruits of a similar kind might be involved in security operations in the Philippines, is being explored in a study at ISDS.[52] For now, the authorities have taken note of this practice and have issued regulations to inhibit the recruitment activities of PMSCs from the regular roster of the police.[53]

Oversight Institutions in the Philippines

Governing the Philippine security sector is an immensely challenging project, not only because of the multiplicity of statutory security actors, but also because of the largely uncontrolled, and more difficult to regulate activities of the non-statutory security actors that are present at the level of the community and the individual. They interface with the population on a daily basis, 24-hours a day, seven days a week, a degree of activity that is not replicated by oversight institutions.

Among the key oversight institutions in the Philippine government are the Office of the President as Commander-in-Chief of the AFP, the National Security Council, various executive departments, legislative committees, a number of independent commissions, and the Ombudsman and Sandiganbayan (fact-finding and prosecutorial body and anti-graft court). Outside of government, societal organisations, such as human rights groups, peace advocates, investigative media, and academic institutions and personalities, also exercise some degree of oversight.

Ensuring that the statutory security actors are put under civilian government oversight mechanisms is part of democratising SSG. In the Philippines, the President is Commander-in Chief of the AFP and sits at the top of the official pyramid of oversight institutions. He/she has the power to appoint top officers in the AFP in conjunction with the legislative Commission on Appointments, a bipartisan body that must endorse the President's choices for the positions of AFP Chief of Staff, the chiefs of the three major service commands, and all promotions from the rank of colonel in the army and air force, and captain in the navy.[54] As head of the National Security Council – a body that includes former presidents and is convened at the pleasure of the incumbent Chief Executive – the President has overarching powers related to national security. The Department of National Defense is the executive department that supervises the AFP, while the PNP, as noted above, is under the Department of the Interior and Local Government. In addition, the police are under oversight by the National Police Commission, one among a number of independent commissions with oversight functions over the statutory security forces. Procurement by the military and the police, as well as related budgetary matters, are under the supervision and examination of the Department of Budget Management, a key actor in the government procurement process, including in the bidding and awards committees of the military and the police.[55]

As already noted, the legislative Commission on Appointments has the power to withhold its confirmation to executive appointments to the highest positions and ranks in the AFP. Confirmation by the legislative Commission on Appointments is necessary in order to effect an executive appointment and promotion of the top ranking military officers. The legislative commissions in both houses of Congress have the power to investigate reported anomalies involving the military and the police, while their committees on the budget can cut or increase budgetary requests that are critical to the proper functioning of the military and the police. In addition to the National Police Commission, that has a wide range of oversight functions over the police, another independent body active in oversight is the Philippine Commission on Human Rights (PCHR). The PCHR provides the military and the police with training in human rights and international humanitarian law, which is a requirement for their promotion, as is a certification from the PCHR that the officer being promoted does not have a case of human rights violation on record. Meanwhile, the Commission on Audit scrutinises expenditures of all government agencies and ensures they follow the applicable law, rules and regulations pertaining to the spending of public funds.

The Ombudsman is the office charged with the power to investigate and prosecute allegations of acts of graft and corruption by high-ranking government officials. It has a deputy that is assigned to look into graft and corruption complaints against the military. When the investigation of a complaint shows probable cause, the Ombudsman files the case before the Sandiganbayan, the country's anti-graft court. At present, there are a number of cases pending before the latter that involve alleged anomalies committed by high-ranking retired military officers. They usually concern financial transactions prejudicial to the government, or unexplained wealth on the part of the accused officers.[56] The conviction rate of the Sandiganbayan depends to a large degree on the ability of prosecutors to produce air-tight evidence against the accused, as well as the extent to which the anti-graft court judges are able to withstand intercession from politically influential personalities in favour of the accused.

Civil society also plays an oversight role for government-based elements of the security sector. Among them are human rights groups and peace advocates. Unfortunately, perhaps due to their origins in the anti-authoritarian protest movements that emerged during the era of martial law, they have not fully availed themselves of the opportunity to engage the state on SSG/SSR issues.[57] Investigative media has also served a similar function. Notable among them is the Philippine Center for Investigative Journalism, whose works – including Glenda Gloria's *We Were Soldiers* – have provided information on statutory security actors that helped galvanise public opinion against the continuing military influence in politics and society. However, this role could be more effective if media could have better access to military and defence information, which is not guaranteed in the current political and legal climate. In this regard, the enactment of a freedom of information law is critical to creating an environment conducive to civil-society oversight. Thus the ongoing SSRI study came up with a tentative conclusion of the same sort when it said that media practitioners consulted by the research team complained about the lack of cooperation from security sector actors, especially the military, in making available basic information that could help make them more effective oversight mechanisms.[58]

In the case of academic institutions and individuals, there is as yet no academic constituency for SSR in the Philippines. There are a few scholars that have looked at democratising civil-military relations, military opinion surveys, conflict resolution and peace studies, as well as political, judicial, police, and military reform, among SSR related issues.[59] ISDS has served as one of the focal points for SSG/SSR in the country and has become a member of global organisations that are looking at SSG/SSR and security transformation, such as the Association of Security Sector Education and Training (ASSET) and the Global Consortium on Security Transformation (GCST). However, an academic constituency for SSG/SSR that can collectively become an oversight mechanism for the statutory security forces and other government agencies that form part of the Philippine security sector has yet to evolve.

SSG in the Philippines: Outstanding Challenges

Improving SSG faces many challenges in the contemporary Philippines. The list that follows is simply indicative, and far from exhaustive:

Challenges associated with political transition: In theory, as provided for by the 1987 constitution and other laws, the foundational principles and frameworks regarding the security sector have already been laid out. These constitutional and legal frameworks include basic principles for democratic governance, such as the supremacy of civilian authority over the military at all times; the functional separation of the police from the military; provisions for civilian oversight by the executive, legislative, and judicial branches of government, as well as in the independent commissions and other government bodies. However, practice leaves much to be desired. For instance, the SSRI study showed that: (1) these constitutional and legal frameworks, as well as specific rules and procedures to perform oversight functions, are not faithfully observed by security sector actors; (2) there is no formal network of oversight institutions, a fact which generates grey areas that could create confusion and overlap among and between them; (3) gaps in civilian oversight remain, such as the exemption of police promotion and appointments from legislative confirmation, as well as the exemption of members of the military and the police deployed for peacekeeping missions abroad; (4) inadequate resources available to the security sector create a gap between expectations and capabilities;[60] and (5) certain policies and laws adopted by the government, such as the Human Security Act on counter-terrorism, have negative implications for good/democratic governance of the security sector.[61]

In addition, the persistence of military influence and participation in politics and society is not conducive to the development of a political environment conducive to good democratic SSG. Democratic control of armed forces posits that the reduction of the military's role in politics is an essential ingredient in the transition from authoritarian rule – where the military was a partner in government, if not the government itself – to democratic rule, where the civilian political authority controls government. Military role expansion has also caused the politicisation of young military officers whose frustration with the civilian government has fuelled several coup attempts in the past.[62]

Challenges associated with conflict and post-conflict situations: The country continues to deal with two domestic armed conflicts in which the military continues to be the principal force used by the government. Reliance on the use of coercion in governance is known to raise the political currency of the military.[63] While domestic armed conflicts continue, and the military remains the government's principal vehicle for stemming them, it is unlikely that the military's political role will diminish.

Moreover, the approach of the government to these conflicts has been incoherent, in so far as it involves three policy positions that do not cohere, and may even work at cross-purposes. These positions are: (1) the pacification position, which seeks a cessation of hostilities while making only enough concessions to the insurgents to bring them to the negotiating table and whose results are generally short lived; (2) the victory position, which seeks the immediate end of armed conflicts and the defeat of the insurgency, accompanied by large-scale violence and repression in violation of human rights, that in the end protracts armed conflict, and fuels and strengthens the insurgency; and (3) the institutional position, which advocates the adoption and implementation of policies necessary to achieve sustainable long-term peace and the creation of institutions to implement and consolidate these policies.[64]

Another important challenge in this regard is the enforcement, as effectively and efficiently as possible, of peace agreements. It bears recalling the claims of Misuari and his MNLF loyalists that the Philippine government failed to implement the peace agreement made with the Ramos administration in 1996. This claim became the basis for the group's rejection of his removal as Governor of the ARMM, as well as Misuari's own defiant stance. Moreover, there is a need to reconcile the military's mission of preventing insurgents from enhancing their forces on the one hand, and on the other, of making the main negotiating partner accountable for their breakaway factions, which continue to undertake recruitment activities under the cover of ceasefire agreements. This is particularly relevant to the peace talks between the MILF and the government. The MILF is known to have breakaway factions whose recruitment activities continued even during the ceasefire agreement with the government. However, the fact that the mission of the military in conflict areas includes the prevention of such activities has led to allegations of AFP violations of the ceasefire whenever they engage these breakaway factions in combat operations.

Finally, in post-conflict situations, the issue of DDR of insurgent forces is a very challenging one.[65] The Philippine experience with the MNLF after the peace agreement was signed in 1996 is illustrative of this challenge. Not only are the issues of the quantity of forces to be disarmed and demobilised, as well as the quality of those to be reintegrated into the regular government forces, already daunting – perhaps a major reason for skipping these phases of DDR and proceeding forthwith to reintegration – but the consequences for the cohesion and effectiveness of the government forces once DDR is being implemented must also be taken into consideration. It is easy to understand how former enemies find it so difficult to develop trust and confidence between themselves. Many confidence-building measures, as well as capacity building activities, for integrated forces need to be undertaken.

Moreover, disarming Muslim secessionist forces is challenged by a socio-religious trait of Muslims that sees the right to bear arms as part of their religious heritage.[66] This was reportedly a major consideration for Misuari and his followers in the decision to go underground when martial law decreed the surrender of firearms to the government.[67]

Challenges that relate to capacity building for security sector actors: Capacity building is a cross-cutting challenge for security sector actors, whether they are statutory security sector actors, government oversight institutions, or civil society oversight actors. Capacity building includes the relevant and appropriate training and education, including in such topics as human rights and international humanitarian law, ethnic and gender sensitivity, and in various other aspects of SSG/SSR. A good example is the imperative for capacity building for legislative committees charged with oversight responsibilities, whose members so far have misperceived, misunderstood, misused, and probably also abused their oversight powers. Even grievance mechanisms to address festering issues of poor performance require capacity building, as well as structural changes.[68]

Challenges that relate to civil society participation: Apart from the general lack of awareness about SSG/SSR among civil society groups or organisations (CSOs) whose areas of concern are relevant to SSG/SSR, such as human rights, peace advocacy, justice, public information, etc., they are also handicapped by a number of other challenges. An important one is attitudinal, that is, a tendency to avoid getting involved in 'security' issues that in the past had been the purview of the military and the police – two institutions of which civil society groups that emerged during authoritarian rule hold a dim view. CSOs and the statutory security forces stood on opposite sides of the government barricades to prevent access by the people to the power-holders during this period. This division has survived the end of martial law.

Another handicap is the natural tendency for 'security' issues to be restricted to the domain of the military, the police, and the intelligence services. However, as this study has argued, since the concept of security is broad, multidimensional, and comprehensive, the statutory security forces ought not to monopolise the provision of security. This should be shared by other relevant actors in the security sector and beyond, and, in fact, must be seen as a 'whole of society' concern. Thus, CSOs need access to accurate information about many of these issues in order to increase their capacity as responsible oversight bodies.

Moreover, there is no network of SSG/SSR advocates that can promote SSG/SSR interests in policy formulation and implementation, as already noted above. Effective action could be achieved with such a network of advocates that can serve as a lobby group in security sector decision-making.

Future Prospects

There is a new administration in the Philippines that has provided an important opportunity for SSR. The new administration is led by the only son of the late Senator Benigno 'Ninoy' Aquino II and the late former President Cory Aquino. 'Noynoy', or President Noynoy (P-Noy), rode on the legacy of his father and the mythology surrounding his mother, the sympathetic feelings of Filipinos for the orphaned, as well as the overwhelming and powerful anti-Gloria Macapagal-Arroyo sentiment of vast numbers of businessmen, public intellectuals and opinion makers, and a broad cross-section of Philippine society. The latter sentiment that continues to inform public discourse, as well as an excuse for the new administration's failings, could be used as a basis for serious and genuine reform efforts, especially of the security sector. P-Noy ran on an anti-corruption platform, a promise he needs to fulfil if his administration is to make a historical imprint on the country's political development.

However, most of the President's men and women are associated with big business interests and political dynasties. These could stand in the way of a serious and genuine reform programme. The way forward is likely to remain as challenging as before and advocates of reform must find reform champions in each of the security sector actors, strategic offices, media, and similar venues to push the SSR agenda. SSR has been adopted as one of the four pillars of national security policy though, and this can be a credible foundation for genuine SSR.

The international development assistance community must be extremely careful with whom they work, and in what areas of reform.

Social investigation, involving a wide array of sources that represent key points in the political spectrum, is critical in this regard.

Notes

1 Samuel P. Huntington, *The Third Wave: Democratization in the Late Twentieth Century* (Norman: University of Oklahoma Press, 1991).

2 This body of literature includes among others, Larry Diamond and Marc Plattner (eds.), *Civil-Military Relations and Democracy* (Baltimore: Johns Hopkins University Press, 1996); Larry Diamond, Marc Plattner, Yun-han Chu, and Hung-mao Tien (eds.), *Consolidating Third Wave Democracies* (Baltimore: Johns Hopkins University Press, 1997); R.J. May and Viberto Selochan (eds.), *The Military and Democracy in Asia and the Pacific* (London: C. Hurst and Co and Bathurst: Crawford House, 1998); Louis W. Goodman, Johanna S.R. Mendelson, and Juan Rial (eds.), *The Military and Democracy: the Future of Civil-Military Relations in Latin America* (Lexington: Lexington Books, 1990); and Rut Diamint (ed.), *Control Civil Y Fuerzas Armadas en Las Nuevas Democracias Latinoamericanas* (Buenos Aires: Nuevohacer para la Universidad Torcuato di Tella, 1994).

3 Security is seen here as comprehensive, multidimensional, and includes the security of both the state and the individual, while development is used in its comprehensive and broad sense to include economic growth and an enabling environment for the achievement of human progress. Security and development are twin concepts that represent the two sides of the coin of human well-being at all levels of governance. See the author's "Linking Security and Development in Southeast Asia: a Concept Paper", in *South East Asia: Security and Stability* (Manila: Konrad-Adenauer Stiftung Philippines Occasional Papers, ca 1995), pp. 33-47.

4 See for example: Ann Fitz-Gerald, "Security Sector Reform – Streamlining National Military Forces to Respond to the Wider Security Needs", *Journal of Security Sector Management*, vol. 1, no. 1, pp. 1-21; and Islam Yusufi, "Understanding the Process of Security Reform in Southeastern Europe", *Journal of Security Sector Management*, vol. 2, no. 2, pp. 1-18.

5 See: OECD, *Security Issues and Development Co-operation: A Conceptual Framework for Enhancing Policy Coherence* (Paris: OECD, 2000); OECD, *Security Sector Reform and Governance: Policy and Good Practice* (Paris: OECD, 2004); and UNDP, "Democratising Security to Prevent Conflict and Build Peace", *Human Development Report 2002: Deepening Democracy in a Fragmented World* (New York and Oxford: Oxford University Press, 2002).

6 See: Nicole Ball, "Transforming Security Sectors: The World Bank and IMF Approaches", *Journal of Conflict, Security and Development*, vol. 1, no. 1, 2001, pp. 45-66; Nicole Ball, Tsjeard Bouta and Luc van de Goor, *Enhancing Democratic Governance of the Security Sector: An Institutional Assessment Framework* (The Hague: Netherlands Institute of International Relations, 2003).

7 ISDS, *Developing a Security Sector Reform Index in the Philippines Towards Conflict Prevention and Peace-Building - Security Sector Reform in the Philippines: A Preliminary Analysis* (Quezon City: Institute for Strategic and Development Studies, 2009).

8 For instance, Jessica Tuchman Mathews wrote about the 'new' meaning of security with the end of the Cold War in her article, "Redefining Security", *Foreign Affairs*, vol. 68, no. 2, 1989, pp. 162-177.

9 See the UNDP, *Human Development Report 1994- New Dimensions of Human Security* (New York and Oxford: Oxford University Press, 1994) for a discussion of the seven categories of human security.

10 The Association of Southeast Asian Nations (ASEAN) and Japan were early advocates of comprehensive security.

11 The idea that security has multiple dimensions, which should be served by different actors, is not well-understood in societies undergoing political transition or conflict, and may therefore lack popular acceptance and support.

12 *Security Sector Governance and Reform*, p. 1.

13 R.A. 7160 – "An Act Providing for the Local Government Code of 1991", dated 10 October 1991.

14 David B. Dewitt and Carolina G. Hernandez (eds.), *Development and Security in Southeast Asia,* volumes I-III (Aldershot, England: Ashgate Publishing Limited, 2003).

15 Hernandez, "Linking Development and Security in Southeast Asia: A Concept Paper".

16 Since 1986, electoral politics have seen the transfer of power from Cory Aquino to Fidel Ramos in 1992, from Ramos to Joseph Estrada in 1998, the election to her own term of Gloria Macapagal-Arroyo in 2004, and from Macapagal-Arroyo to Benigno Aquino III in May 2010.

17 These incidents were the OPLAN Hackle of February 2006 and the associated Manila Peninsula Incident.

18 For a full account of these coup attempts, especially that of 29 December 1989, see *The Final Report of the Fact-Finding Commission pursuant to R.A. No. 6832, October 1990* (Makati: Bookmark, Inc., 1990).

19 Glenda Gloria has documented the increasing number of appointments of retired military officers in strategic agencies in the executive departments of government, including the cabinet from the years of the Cory Aquino administration to the early years of the Macapagal-Arroyo administration in her work, *We Were Soldiers: Military Men in Politics and the Bureaucracy* (Makati City: Friedrich Ebert Stiftung, 2003).

20 Human Development Network, *Philippine Human Development Report 2005—Peace, Human Security and Human Development in the Philippines* (Manila: HDN in cooperation with UNDP and NZAID, 2005).

21 Table 1.1 Provinces with the highest number of armed encounters (1986-2004), in *ibid.*, p. 2.

22 Table 4.12 Provinces versus countries (province HDI figures for 2003, country figures for 2003), in *ibid.*, p. 105.

23 Box 2.4 Counting costs of the protracted war in Southern Philippines 1969-1996, in *ibid.*, p. 72.

24 On these case studies, see further ISDS, *Developing a Security Sector Reform Index in the Philippines*, pp. 100-121 for Bohol and pp.121-153 for Leon, Iloilo.

25 *Ibid.*

26 An account of the historical development of the country's military and police is found in Carolina G. Hernandez, *The Extent of Civilian Control of the Military in the Philippines: 1946-1976*, an unpublished doctoral dissertation, State University of New York at Buffalo, 1979, Chapters 3 and 4. Available at University Microfilms, University of Michigan at Ann Arbor, 1980.

27 The provision of external security by US forces came to a formal end with the removal of US forces from Philippine military bases in 1991 when a successor treaty to the US-Philippine Military Bases Agreement was rejected by the Philippine Senate.

28 The Philippine Defense Reform program adopted during the Macapagal-Arroyo administration was guided by the strategic view that in the short to medium term, the country's security challenges would be domestic insurgency and ethnic separatism. Thus, the AFP was trained to improve its internal defense capability, and the Philippine National Police Law that assigned the internal security function to the police was not fully implemented. To date, the military remains primarily responsible for the counterinsurgency function.

29 See for example, John Gershman, "Is Southeast Asia the Second Front?", *Foreign Affairs*, vol. 81, no. 4, July-August 2003, pp. 60-74, and Amitav and Arabinda Acharya, "The Myth of the Second Front: Localizing the 'War on Terror' in Southeast Asia", *The Washington Quarterly*, vol. 3, no. 4, Autumn 2007, pp. 75-90.

30 The Huks were a non-statutory security actor for the Philippine peasantry in the areas they controlled, primarily in Luzon, from the late 1940s to the early 1950s. A vivid account of how absentee landlordism contributed immensely to the Huk insurgency is found in Benedict J. Kerkvliet, *The Huk Rebellion: A Study of Peasant Revolt in the Philippines* (Berkeley: University of California Press, 1977).

31 For details of this process of integration with, and separation of, the police from the military over time, see Hernandez, *The Extent of Civilian Control of the Military in the Philippines: 1946-1976*, Chapter 3.

32 See Ed Quitoriano and Ed Libre, "Reaching for the Gun: The Human Cost of Small Arms in Central Mindanao", *Kasarinlan, A Philippine Journal of Third World Studies*, vol. 16, no. 2, 2001, pp. 27-28. This article is also a useful source of other armed groups and arms supplies in the Philippines.

33 See the findings of the SSRI Project in ISDS, *Developing a Security Sector Reform Index in the Philippines*, p. 154.

34 See for examples, Robert Weissman, Recent Development: "Development" and the Denial of Human Rights in Ramos's Philippines", *Harvard Human Rights*

Journal, vol. 7, 1994, pp. 251-263; Human Rights Watch, *Scared Silent: Impunity for Extrajudicial Killings in the Philippines*, vol. 19, no.9(C), June 2007, http://www.hrw.org/reports/2007/philippines0607/philippines0607web.pdf; and Amnesty International, *Philippines: Political Killings, Human Rights and the Peace Process*, August 15, 2006.

35 On the origins of the new CPP and NPA, see Francisco Nemenzo, "Rectification Process and the Philippine Communist Movement", in Lim Joo-Jock and Vani S. (eds.), *Armed Communist Movements in Southeast Asia* (Singapore: Institute of Southeast Asian Studies, 1984).

36 The MILF is the successor Muslim separatist group to the Moro National Liberation Front (MNLF) led by Nur Misuari. An account of the rise of the MNLF is found in Eliseo Mercado, "Culture, Economics and Revolt in Mindanao: The Origins of the MNLF and the Politics of Moro Separatism", in Lim Joo-Jock and Vani S. (eds.), *Armed Separatism in Southeast Asia* (Singapore: Institute of Southeast Asian Studies, 1985), pp. 151-175. For a comprehensive analysis of Muslim separatism in Mindanao, see Patricio N. Abinales, "Sancho Panza in Buliok Complex: The Paradox of Muslim Separatism", in Rodolfo C. Severino and Lorraine Carlos Salazar (eds.), *Whiter the Philippines in the 21st Century?* (Singapore: Institute of Southeast Asian Studies and Konrad-Adenaeur Stiftung, 2007), pp. 277-312.

37 A study of the PMSC phenomenon in the Philippines was conducted by Katherine Marie G. Hernandez, "The Engagement of Foreign Private Military and Security Corporations in the Philippines: An Exploratory Study" as part of the Working Group on the Privatization of Security under the Global Consortium on Security Transformation (GCST) coordinated by FLACSO-Chile, August 2010. See also her article on "Private Military and Security Corporations in the Philippines: Towards a Comprehensive Security Sector Reform Program", *The Indonesian Quarterly*, vol. 39, no.1, 2011, pp. 21-34.

38 This present insurgency is in its fourth decade, although its forerunner, the Huk insurgency began in late 1940 and lasted until the early 1950s. On the present communist insurgency, see Alexander R. Magno, "The Insurgency That Would Not Go Away", in Severino and Salazar (eds.), *Whither the Philippines in the 21st Century*, pp. 313-329.

39 The present President Benigno S. Aquino III has initiated peace talks with the CPP-NPA-NDF and resumed talks with the MILF. The adviser for the peace process hopes to attain peace within three years.

40 Curiously, the cell sites of one major service provider has not experienced any such attack, leading to suspicions that it must be paying the NPA protection money on a regular basis.

41 Fieldwork for the case study of Bohol Province in the ISDS project on developing a security sector index for the Philippines documents this practice by the NPA. The researchers were shown copies of receipts issued by the NPA for the 'payment' of 'permit to campaign' fees in cash or in kind.

42 Abinales, "Sancho Panza in Buliok Complex", Table 12.1 MILF Affected Barangays (Last Quarter 2005), p. 283.

43 Malcolm Cook and Kit Collier, *Mindanao: A Gamble Worth Taking*, Lowy Institute Paper 17 (Double Bay, New South Wales: Longview Media, 2006), p. 11.

44 *Ibid.*

45 Quitoriano and Libre, "Reaching for the Gun", pp. 26-27

46 International Crisis Group (ICG), *The Philippine Counter-Insurgency vs. Counter-Terrorism in Mindanao*, Asia Report No. 152 - 13 May 2008 (Jakarta/Brussels: ICG, 13 May 2008), p. 3.

47 The complex relationship between and among the Muslim secessionist groups can be seen in *ibid.*, pp. 3-20. The Report argues that unless the government recognises the importance of a key element in the ASG's decline – i.e., intelligence sharing on terrorists with the MILF and avoidance of accidental clashes while pursuing the ASG – the positive result of the AFP's classic counterinsurgency formula against the ASG could be short-lived.

48 For an illustration of the role of the MNLF breakaway wing in the dynamics of Muslim secessionism in Mindanao, see *ibid.*

49 On the implementation of post-conflict agreements with the MNLF, see Merliza Makinano and Alfredo Lubang, "Disarmament, Demobilization and Reintegration: The Mindanao Experience", in Dipankar Banerjee (ed.), *South Asia at Gun Point: Small Arms and Light Weapons Proliferation* (Colombo: Regional Center for Strategic Studies, 2000). For Philippine experiences with non-statutory security actors, see Soliman M. Santos, Jr. and Paz Verdades M. Santos (eds.), *Primed and Purposeful: Armed Groups and Human Security Efforts in the Philippines* (Geneva: Small Arms Survey, Graduate Institute of International and Development Studies, April 2010). A government perspective is given by former Presidential Adviser on the Peace Process, Avelino I. Razon, Jr., "The Philippines' Experience on Reintegration Program and the GRP's Emerging Policy on DDR", in Office of the Presidential Adviser on the Peace Process (OPAP) and United Nations Development Programme (UNDP), *Discourses, Views and Experiences on Disarmament, Demobilization and Reintegration: International and Local Perspectives* (Benzel Z Press, Inc., 2009), pp. 51-65.

50 In general, assessments on the outcome of the peace agreement between the MNLF and the Philippine government tend to portray a flawed implementation process, which has not led to sustainable peace and development. See for example, Francisco J. Lara Jr. and Phil Champain, "Inclusive Peace in Muslim Mindanao: Revisiting the Dynamics of Conflict and Exclusion", *International Alert*, June 2009, http://www.international-alert.org/sites/default/files/publications/Inclusive_Peace_in_Muslim_Mindanao_Revisiting_the_dynamics_of_conflict_and_exclusion.pdf

51 From a private source interviewed by the author.

52 Hernandez, "The Engagement of Foreign Military and Security Corporations in the Philippines", August 2010.

53 From a private source interviewed by the author.

54 Sec. 18, Article VI, 1987 Philippine Constitution.

55 This authority is provided for in the Government Procurement Act of January 2003 and its Implementing Rules and Regulations (RA 9184 and IRR-A).

56 Among the widely publicised cases are those involving retired officers who ran the Retirement Services and Benefits System set up by Marcos, which failed to evolve into a pension system for the military, and the cases filed against a former AFP Comptroller that allegedly amassed huge amounts of unexplained wealth. On the Retirement Services and Benefits System, see *The Report of the Fact-Finding Commission Pursuant to Administrative Order No. 78 of the President of the Republic of the Philippines Dated July 30, 2003* (Manila: Feliciano Commission, 17 October 2003).

57 See: Aries A. Arugay, "Civil Society and Security Sector Reform (SSR) in the Philippines," *Indonesian Quarterly*, vol. 35, no. 4, Fourth Quarter 2007, pp. 344-358.

58 ISDS, *Developing a Security Sector Reform Index for the Philippines*, pp. 58-59.

59 Among them are the present author, Felipe B. Miranda and Ruben Ciron, Francisco Nemenzo, Jr, Patricio Abinales, Alexander R. Magno, Herman J.S. Kraft, Miriam Coronel-Ferrer, Aries A. Arugay, Raymund Quilop, Ma. Serena Diokno, and Renato de Castro.

60 ISDS, *Developing a Security Sector Reform Index in the Philippines*, pp. 53-58.

61 *Ibid.*, p. 155.

62 Carolina G. Hernandez, "Restoring Democratic Civilian Control over the Philippine Military: Challenges and Prospects", *Journal of International Cooperation Studies*, vol. 10, no. 1, June 2002, pp. 25-48.

63 Muthiah Alagappa, "Asian Civil-Military Relations: Key Developments, Explanations, and Trajectories", in Muthiah Alagappa (ed.), *Coercion and Governance: The Declining Political Role of the Military in Asia* (Stanford: Stanford University Press, 2001), pp. 452-453.

64 Paul Oquist in a 2002 paper as cited in Carolina G. Hernandez, "The AFP's institutional responses to armed conflict: a continuing quest for the right approach", *PIDS Policy Notes* No. 2006-02 (March 2006), p. 2. The original was a background paper for the *2005 Philippine Human Development Report.*

65 Merliza M. Makinano and Alfredo Lubang, *Disarmament, Demobilization and Reintegration: The Mindanao Experience* (Ottawa: Department of Foreign Affairs and International Trade, February 2001).

66 *Ibid.*, p. 15.

67 Mercado, "Culture, Economics and Revolt in Mindanao".

68 ISDS, *Developing a Security Sector Reform Index in the Philippines*, pp. 59-84, and pp. 154-155.

3 *Crossing the Threshold: Thailand's Path to Rethinking Security Sector Governance*

KEOKAM KRAISORAPHONG

Thailand has struggled to reconcile its identity as a nation that has achieved continuous economic development in the past several decades, with its nature as an ever more deeply divided society, evidenced in the political developments of the past few years. Thailand's security sector has been put under much stress and increased pressure since the recurrence of the violent conflict in the Deep South in 2001. More recently, public demands on the security sector, particularly the military, to take a stand in resolving the escalated violence, as well as the political conflict manifested in the April-May 2010 crisis, have varied and left many in doubt of the security institutions' position, and not least of its efficiency and effectiveness in matters of security sector governance (SSG). The crisis prompted the Thai people to realise how polarised their political aspirations had become, while on the other hand, also raising serious questions regarding the future of Thailand's democratisation and its implications for SSG in Thailand.

Through an examination of the worst situation of violence that Thailand has ever witnessed and the gravest crisis that has put Thailand's security sector to the test, this chapter seeks to explain Thailand's SSG. The chapter's focus on the Thai context will reflect how Thailand's security sector functions under a political power structure, which has come to be challenged by social change manifested in a radical social movement that has set the recent political conflict in motion. In fact, while the violence from the conflict in Southern Thailand has received the most attention due to it being a much more internationalised and more highly publicised case –

especially in its connection with notions of terrorism – this analysis will suggest that it is but a reflection of the security sector's role in a much larger challenge to Thailand's political power structure. The nature of the political power structure and the fact that it dictates Thailand's SSG is most obviously reflected in the recent political crisis.

This chapter discusses how the circumstances of the continued political conflict may provide a window of opportunity for Thailand to rethink its perspectives on SSG. It argues that given the overarching political power structure and the sensitivity of the situation, any reform of the Thai security sector will not be open to external intervention, but must instead be endogenous to the process of political change.

Thailand's SSG: The Pivotal Role of the Military

The military, and its long-standing involvement in Thai socio-political affairs, features prominently in Thailand's SSG. Since the end of absolute monarchy in 1932, and the advent of constitutional monarchy, Thailand has experienced intervals of military intervention – the latest in September 2006 being the eighteenth coup d'état. Studies of Thai civil-military relations, which explain the predominant role of the Thai military in the security sector and illustrate its long-standing involvement in state affairs, have been extensively undertaken and extremely well articulated in the work of Beeson and Bellamy, among several other scholars.[1] This chapter will discuss five periods of military intervention, which are of particular relevance for the purpose of understanding Thailand's political power structure.

The first period of significance was marked by the coup which ended absolute monarchy in 1932 and which was a turning point where the military shifted from being "unquestioning(ly) subservient to monarchical rule"[2], in order to resume a role it defined for itself as custodian of the new constitutional regime and Thai democracy.[3] It was during this period that cooperation between the bureaucracy and the military sprang out of common interests and ideology. The alliance was based on their shared values of Thai nationalism and anti-communism. After the Second World War, royalism became another particular element among these shared values.[4] Democratisation was limited by the military's control over government, which it used to legitimate its role with reference to democracy and nationalism.

The second period took the form of a transition of power within the military through a coup led by Field Marshal Sarit Thanarat in 1958. Notable under Sarit's rule was the shift from constitutionalism to a "new paternalistic system justified by reference to the monarchy".[5] While this allowed Sarit to maintain his dictatorship in that era, it has also since become a system that legitimises the military's involvement in most affairs of the Thai state (a point that will be elaborated further in later discussions of Thailand's political power structure). The remaining importance of nationalism and anti-communism notwithstanding, Sarit's consolidation of power through the legitimacy associated with monarchism and economic development was reinforced by the support of a significant portion of the capitalist and middle classes, who were tied to the regime by the interests vested in "their social position, access to resources and protection from other social forces"[6] provided by the power of the state. But this shift came at the expense of a weakening civil-military coalition.[7] Sarit's authoritarian government embarked on a 'development for security' programme with external aid from its ally, the United States, and led Thailand into a period marked by "the relationship between government, army and society and the centrality of economic development to the state's legitimacy"[8] (which will be discussed in more detail in the later part of this chapter, which focuses on the nexus between security and development). A full-scale student-led revolt against direct military rule in 1973 and the political turmoil that ensued throughout the 1970s notwithstanding, the military was still entrusted to fight against communist insurgents, and to play an increasingly important role in economic development.[9] The assembly, appointed by the king to provide a pathway towards democratisation following the 1973 revolt, proved futile in achieving a transition to democracy.

The 1977 coup, staged by young military officers, marks the third period. With the idea that the military's principal political role was to prepare the nation for "transition to democratic rule",[10] the coup set the stage for the government's declaration in 1980 that democratisation was the best way to defeat communism.[11] By the late 1980s, the communist threat had waned to a non-issue, while civilian control of the military had become increasingly entrenched because of the strong support liberal political parties were able to establish with civil society and more importantly with the business community. At the same time, this state of affairs in civil-military relations was taking a turn for the worse, as a deep divide between reformists and traditionalists within the military became more evident.

The fourth period began in the early 1990s: when the government acted on its mandate to tighten civilian control over the military and pursued a military restructuring policy, the traditionalist faction of the military responded with a coup in 1992. But failing to legitimate its return to power, the military eventually lost the support of the middle class it had earlier enjoyed. Also, the eventual call for elections in an attempt to re-legitimate military rule resulted in a massive civilian uprising. A violent military crackdown resulted in a number of deaths, which marked the beginning of a significant decline in the military's role in politics that lasted for more than a decade. During that period, revisions of the major laws, which had been instrumental in the military's claim on extraordinary powers in crisis situations, were reduced, putting the armed forces in its place as a state instrument.[12] Cabinet authorisation was required for use of military forces in riot control, a mission which was then transferred to the police.[13]

The fifth and most recent period of military intervention began with the September 2006 coup, and occurred at a time when the deep divide in Thai society had also begun to reveal itself. The coup-makers justified their seizure of power with "allegations of corruption and abuse of power by the Thaksin government, and claims that Thaksin had acted disrespectfully towards the monarchy".[14] Under Thaksin's premiership (between 2001 and September 2006), politicisation of the military was entrenched, as Thaksin set out to install his allies in strategic positions. What seemingly was civilian control over the military under a democratic regime was in actual fact the political manoeuvring of the government in the service of its own interests so as to strengthen its power base for political domination.[15] However, the 1997 constitution – known as the peoples' constitution and the most democratic constitution Thailand has ever had – was abrogated by the Council for National Security (CNS), which was established by the coup group to oversee drafting and ratification of the 2007 constitution. The 2007 election which followed was to mark the beginning of a long and eventually violent rivalry between the People's Alliance for Democracy (PAD), known as the 'Yellow Shirts', and the United Front of Democracy Against Dictatorship (UDD), known as the 'Red Shirts'.

As Beeson and Bellamy point out, the Royal Thai Army for the most part of its history has been "the pre-eminent state institution and has seen its primary role as that of a nation-builder".[16] Its prominent role in suppressing communist insurgencies and in protecting the Thai borders against external threats legitimated its deep involvement in state affairs during the period of the Cold War. The military's extended effort to establish "a particular vision of Thai national identity"[17] and to lead Thailand's economic development also enabled it to establish networks with its civilian counterparts, and coalitions with politicians and business leaders that have further strengthened its roots in Thailand's political power structure. More importantly, the military's pledge of allegiance to the monarchy, established during Sarit's time, continues to be a key resource through which the military legitimates its acts "by direct appeal to the authority of the king",[18] adamantly insisting that regime security and national security are Thailand's first priority. Another channel by which the military has commonly sought to legitimate itself is by "invoking the rhetoric of democracy and handing over to civilian allies",[19] as has been widely observed by the Thai public in the case of the 2008 Democrat-led coalition government.

The Nexus between Security and Development

Thailand's first link to the international development system occurred in the late 1950s under Sarit's attempt to legitimise his rule by shifting from the use of nationalism and anti-communism as the government's social bases of legitimacy to economic development and monarchism.[20] Established relationships with external agencies – primarily the World Bank and the US Agency for International Development (USAID) – provided an important basis of foreign financial and technical resources, which included policy advisors. With the strengthening of the legal framework for development and the creation of an organisational base to serve as the planning and implementing institutions for policy technocrats, the military, as "the state's principal bureaucratic arm",[21] was tasked with spearheading national economic development, most notably in poverty-stricken rural areas susceptible to communist opposition.

In this sense, economic development provided a key means of overseeing internal security, and no other institution was more suitable to deliver economic development to these sensitive rural areas than the military. As a number of institutions[22] were created to accomplish the government's 'development for security' programme, the military's influence in the national economy was essentially expanded by its broadened and deepened control of rural areas deemed vulnerable to communism: its task was to direct and coordinate projects to drive economic development in those areas.[23] The Thai military's role in development has been carved out with an overriding security rationale and has thus long been recognised as part of its engagement with Thai society.

Thailand in the 1970s and early 1980s saw the role of the Thai military become ever more prominent, as it gained "more freedom of manoeuvre to tackle the internal threat of communism".[24] While economic management was becoming more complex, recurrent political unrest during much of the 1970s shocked the system, causing, for example, seven cabinet reshuffles during one five-year development plan alone.[25] This was a major distraction for the governments in power, who thus showed little interest in development plans or the planning machinery, instead counting on policy technocrats and the military to carry on the tasks of economic development.

However, by the late 1980s as the communist threat became a non-issue, Thailand saw increasingly entrenched civilian control of the military. At the same time, the importance of the private sector's role increased as Thailand embarked on a decade-long economic boom.[26] During the years to follow, liberal political parties were able to establish strong support within civil society and more importantly with the business community.

It is, however, important to note that despite the recognition in earlier development plans of how rapid economic growth had generated new inequalities, Thailand's economic success during its decade-long boom had masked the fact that Thailand's public policy had not paid sufficient attention to a "number of problems that would not resolve themselves through further benign neglect".[27] This became evident in what is widely believed to be one of the root causes of the 2010 political conflict. Today, it could be said that when the notion of internal security is linked to any form of development, the Thai military remains a significant player – such as in the case of Southern Thailand. A further example is in the case of border-related development, seen in trade with neighbouring countries, where power continues to be vested in military governments and where the Thai military is heavily relied upon for their military-to-military relations with these governments.

The Four Dimensions of Thailand's Security Sector

This chapter is "premised upon a state-centric view of security and the state's monopoly over the legitimate means of coercion",[28] which does reflect how the Thai security sector is commonly perceived. Viewed in terms of the four dimensions of the security sector, Thailand could represent a lopsided security sector with the security forces, particularly the military, dominating among the four dimensions of SSG.[29]

Against the Thai military's firm grip on the security sector, legitimised both by the circumstances of the situation during each period and by the military's own strategies – as has been reviewed above – the other three dimensions of the security sector appear to have always remained marginalised. In terms of oversight mechanisms, observations indicate that "the Thai parliament has not yet taken any steps to empower itself to be an informed and authoritative actor concerning military affairs".[30] While an Armed Forces Committee is present in each of both houses, it has been pointed out that "they are not institutionalised".[31] More importantly, due to their lack of technical capacity in military and security affairs, they are without the competence to engage in any meaningful debate with regards to military affairs.[32] It has thus been come to pass that "military affairs are left out of the legislative branch".[33] This fact is affirmed by the suggestion that the Thai parliament's lack of military expertise has "permitted the military to avoid proper subjugation to civilian and democratic scrutiny".[34] This lack of military expertise has left the parliament without the capacity to scrutinise defence policy, despite its formal right to do so.[35]

Even in terms of non-state oversight institutions, civil society at large is known to avoid discussion of military matters, the primary reason being their lack of the technical expertise necessary to initiate or engage in such debates.[36] Other reasons that have been cited include the lack of strong participatory institutions more generally. Institutions such as the National Human Rights Commission, the Ombudsman, and the Anti-corruption Agency, were only established under the 1997 constitution.

The lack of civil society involvement, and its implications for Thailand's SSG, stem from the "absence of informed public debate" within Thai civil society.[37] As this is seen to have "encouraged the military to maintain its practical autonomy", it indicates the failure of civil society to "create a normative context conducive to military professionalisation".[38] Without public scrutiny the government has been able to "pursue its policy of military control through politicisation".[39]

So, if from a democratic SSG point of view, the challenge of SSG is "to develop both effective oversight mechanisms and affordable security bodies capable of providing security for the state and its citizens on the basis of democratic governance",[40] then the lack of expertise and involvement along the other three dimensions of the security sector – non-state security providers and state and non-state oversight institutions – is indeed part of such a challenge for Thailand's SSG. More importantly, the civilian government's policy of military control through politicisation has made it that much more difficult for civil-military relations to develop towards meaningful reform of the security sector.

To further illustrate the above analysis, the four dimensions of the Thai security sector will be reflected throughout the following two cases examining the challenges to Thailand's SSG. They are the cases that have put Thailand's security sector to test and remain Thailand's preeminent security concerns for this decade: the violent conflict in Southern Thailand, and the recent political conflict, which led to violence in April-May 2010.

Challenges of Thailand's SSG

The unfolding of two violent conflict situations during this past decade has brought Thailand's security sector to international attention, while at the same time bringing to the fore the many SSG challenges Thailand faces.

The Southern Conflict

The roots of the Southern Thai conflict (mainly in three provinces: Pattani, Yala, and Narathiwat) can be traced back historically nearly half a century. With a population that is 80 per cent Malay-speaking and Muslim, the three southernmost provinces of Thailand have been under Bangkok's assimilation and standardisation policy for most of their history. Known for a long tradition of resistance to Bangkok's rule, these three provinces have been marked by political violence during various periods. Guerrilla war against the state began in the 1960s and became most acute between the late 1970s and early 1980s. However, governments between 1980-1988 successfully contained the violence with new security and governance arrangements for the area established and coordinated by the Southern Border Provinces Administrative Centre (SBPAC), which was created for this purpose. These security and governance arrangements muted the violence for two decades, before the latest outburst of violence, which started in 2001, according to government reports.[41] As of April 2008, it has been reported that 3,002 people have been killed and 4,871 injured.[42]

This resurgence of a long-dormant Malay-Muslim resentment against the central government has drawn much attention from the academic and security communities, partly with respect to the question of why ethnic violence, especially post-2004, has become more acute, and whether this trend is in any way indicative of links to *Jemaah Islamiyah* (JI) and to the broader global jihadist network. More recently, studies have argued that the localised and nationalist nature of the conflict has apparently not changed, despite the fact that many of the attacks perpetrated in the three southern provinces do have religious elements.[43] But the "extremely strong sense of Malay-Muslim self-identity" is seen as a "built-in barrier" that would make any penetration by a group such as JI extremely difficult.[44] However, the possibility that this could change is believed to depend on two conditions: firstly, an influx of Talibanised religious radicals that could persuade their local counterparts to make their struggle more relevant to the Muslim world through the link with broader Islamist goals; and, secondly, the enhancement of Thai–US security collaboration that could increase foreign internal defence aid to provide the Royal Thai Army with further resources for their operations in the southern provinces.[45]

Apart from the focus on the religious element of the conflict, Croissant has argued that the factors which account for the recent increase in violence are the "recent Islamisation of Muslim minority identity, policy failures of the sitting government and low quality conflict management".[46] These factors are seen to have provided new opportunities and heightened incentives within "the structural and situational environment in which violent actors have to act".[47] This kind of enabling environment lies within a broad grey zone where criminals and terrorists are not clearly distinguished but their presence is signalled by the prevalence of organised and petty crime, the small-arms trade, smuggling, and drug trafficking, all of which provide fertile ground for what Croissant terms "entrepreneurs of violence".[48]

Noting the lack of rule of law and the lack of efficient law enforcement, some have noted that countering separatist insurgence in southern Thailand has become increasingly difficult, as certain groups have over time come to capitalise on the crisis through budget allocations and the arms trade. In order to sustain their gains, those with vested interests have been known to perpetuate violence at the expense of progress towards peaceful co-existence and a more stable and secure environment.[49] Yet, the understanding that the root of the conflict "revolves around perceptions of ethno-religious alienation, discrimination, and marginalisation", [50] has led most studies to conclude that the resolution of this conflict will come not through the use of force, but rather through "a far more nuanced and multifaceted civic educational-oriented approach than the central government has traditionally been prepared to enact".[51]

McCargo, on the other hand, contends that the Thai Southern conflict is a test "establishing the legitimacy of the Chakri dynasty", whereby the violence, which has resurged since 2001, is the result of Thaksin's "assault on the legitimacy of the palace".[52] Seeking to displace the Democrat-network of the monarchy so that he might incorporate the Southern provinces into his own network, Thaksin in mid-2002 abolished the SBPAC, established in 1981 by the government of the former military Prime Minister, Prem Tinsulanond. The SBPAC represented a set of security and governance arrangements seen to have curtailed the violence for two decades by way of employing "the mode of virtuous rule", underpinned by the "network monarchy", which comprises an extensive network of lieutenants and supporters. [53] The consequences of abolishing the SBPAC were compounded by Thaksin's move to make the police responsible for law and order – as the police were known to constitute "a substantial security problem in the deep South" where they were "so widely disliked and mistrusted".[54]

The Krue Se Siege of 28 April 2004, and the 25 October 2004 Takbai incident exemplified the Thaksin administration's misuse of repressive measures in response to the extensive violent rebellion it faced.[55] The 2005 emergency decree, which gave the security sector broad authority to use force against and detain suspected Islamic insurgents in the three Southern provinces, was judged by critics as significantly limiting individuals' constitutional rights. Although a National Reconciliation Commission (NRC) was set up[56] in March 2005, not much materialised from the effort due to both Thaksin's lack of intention to implement the Committee's recommendations, as well as the fact that the Committee's proposals were deemed "too progressive by most government officials but did not go nearly far enough for most Malay Muslims".[57]

According to McCargo, politics of the Deep South is in many respects "a microcosm of the wider power struggles affecting Thailand".[58] Such wider power struggles were in fact also seen to unfold in the violent political conflict of 2010.

The Political Conflict and Violence of Thailand's Deep Divide

After the September 2006 coup, political conflict again became manifest when the 2007 election under the 2007 constitution brought to power a coalition government led by the pro-Thaksin, People's Power Party (PPP). The PPP's constitutional amendment plan had prompted the PAD (Yellow Shirts) to reconvene their protest movement. The protest escalated to the seizure of the Government House and eventually to the seizure and closure of Suvarnabhumi Airport, Bangkok's main international airport. This only came to an end when the Constitutional Court announced its verdict to dissolve the PPP, and to ban its executive board from political office, after finding it guilty of election fraud. As the Constitutional Court had already brought down two consecutive pro-Thaksin prime ministers, the Democrat-led coalition government's rise to rule through the formation of a coalition government, partly with newly registered parties reconstituted from the dissolved PPP, was rejected by former PPP members and their Red Shirt supporters. Thus their protest against the Democrat-led coalition government began in April 2009 when the Fourth ASEAN Summit was disrupted in a violent confrontation of the Red Shirts with security forces and the Blue Shirt government supporters. It was at this point that the government declared a state of emergency.

This series of events took place from the beginning of 2010 and developed into a prolonged anti-government protest that lasted from March–May 2010. In response to the unrest, the government decreed a new Internal Security Act in March and declared the state of emergency in the second week of April, forbidding any political assemblies of more than five people. At this time the Centre for the Administration of Peace and Order under the Internal Security Operations Command (ISOC) was transformed into the Centre for the Resolution of the Emergency Situation (CRES), in order to function as a special operations centre.[59] But as the protest extended to a second site in downtown Bangkok, the government's unsuccessful attempt to regain control of the first protest site led to a violent confrontation on April 10, which resulted in 25 deaths and more than 800 injuries.[60]

The tug of war between the government and the UDD proceeded while a number of civil society groups appealed to both sides to seek a non-violent resolution through peaceful means and negotiations to resolve the conflict.[61] As the government rejected the UDD's proposal to end the protests on the condition that the government agrees to dissolve parliament within 30 days and hold elections, it became clear that the government had no intention of backing down. Instead the government further responded by publicly claiming that the anti-government protests were founded on a plan to overthrow the monarchy. The CRES published a diagram, which purported to draw links between those allegedly involved in the plan. But failing to generate any public support for its claim, the government changed course, proposing to dissolve parliament in September so as to hold an election in November under the terms of a 'peaceful roadmap'.[62] However, unsettled issues of accountability for protest-related violence led the UDD to back away from the proposed roadmap and to refuse the government's demand to immediately abandon the protest site.[63] The government claimed that terrorists were nested amongst the Red-Shirt protesters and announced its decision to crack down on the movement. As of the 19 May crackdown, the violence linked to this political conflict had caused 88 deaths and left more than 1,885 wounded,[64] including foreign journalists and medical workers.[65]

As the CRES declared that many parts of Thailand remained unstable, the government extended the use of the Emergency Decree on Public Administration in Emergency Situations, B.E. 2548 (2005), under which the CRES continued as the main agency responsible for security-related matters. It was not until 21 December 2010 that a cabinet decision lifted the Emergency Decree, replacing it with the Internal Security Act (ISA) and, as a result, dissolving the CRES.

Thailand's Post-Conflict Peacebuilding

The relevance of security governance issues, such as security sector reform (SSR), to the tasks of peacebuilding is premised on the notion that lasting peace depends on both the state and its population's security needs being equally addressed in parallel with political and socio-economic considerations.[66] As peacebuilding is a conflict-sensitive approach, it is an instrument that could be employed for the purposes of conflict prevention or management, as well as post-conflict reconstruction.[67]

Thailand's effort in peacebuilding has thus far been in post-conflict situations, as seen in the NRC, an independent body set up by the government to address the violent Southern conflict. Three committees were also established to address the violent political conflict of 2010: the Committee on Reform Strategy, the Committee on Reform Assembly, and the Fact-finding Committee.

The NRC was an unprecedented initiative in Thailand, set up in March 2005.[68] According to McCargo "most members of the NRC could not be seen as representatives of the various parties to the conflict, and two-thirds of them were from outside the Southern region".[69] The bulk of the work in detail was done by six sub-committees: Truth, Justice and Human Rights; Conflict Management through Peaceful Means; Development Approaches for Human Security; Power of Cultural Diversity in Thai Society; Unity and Reconciliation in the Area; and Communication with Society.[70]

In a report of June 2006, the NRC proposed modest measures to improve "the quality of justice, security, and governance".[71] This contributed to criticism of the Commission and its performance as "too unwieldy, conservative and timid to firmly address the causes of the crisis, the question of agency, and the need for a political settlement".[72] According to McCargo, a few factors have contributed to this lost opportunity: too large a number of Commission members, a lack of trust and openness, the perception that the political dimensions of the conflict were off-limits, and a failure to engage with the core questions underpinning the violence.[73]

Also, it is important to note that despite the NRC's emphasis on issues of justice, the security community remained in favour of tough legal measures from the perspective that "the violence remained essentially a security problem".[74] It was deemed necessary "to confront the problem head-on" by the use of the 2005 emergency decree or "the systematic arrest of 'ringleaders' and front-line militants".[75] Eventually it became evident that the NRC was divided in its approach to the Southern conflict between those who perceived the crisis to be essentially a political problem on the one hand, and on the other hand those who were adamant that it was essentially a security problem.[76] However, most members of the NRC[77] were noted to view the crisis as a political problem basically involving matters of "justice, equity, identity and governance" – that together "demanded a rethinking of Thailand's ethnic relations", which would require "a more nuanced understanding of Islam, and recognition of Pattani's distinctive history and cultural differences".[78]

As a result of the April-May 2010 violence and following the government's reconciliation plan, in early July the cabinet approved the Regulation of the Office of the Prime Minister to establish two committees: a 19-member Committee on Reform Strategy,[79] and a 27-member Committee on Reform Assembly.[80] The mandate of both committees is to start a reform process that as part of the government's reconciliation plan would address the structural problems related to economic and social disparity. While both committees are to work in coordination, they will each take a different focus over the next three years.[81]

The Committee on Reform Strategy is to focus on the drafting of reform strategies, measures and processes, as well as the formulation of recommendations for government and public consideration. In contrast, the Committee on Reform Assembly is to concentrate on encouraging public participation in the reform process. This involves establishing a national level assembly and supporting the creation of lower level assemblies relevant to specific issues and localities. Together, the two committees are to address areas of necessary reform, which could range from the social value system to the social welfare system.[82]

The government had earlier appointed a Truth and Reconciliation Commission,[83] intended to be an independent fact-finding committee, to conduct a two-year investigation into the May killings. However, many have questioned the impartiality and independence of the committee, since the Committee Chair, rather than coming from a "transparent selection process involving academics, human rights groups and the broader civil society", was instead appointed by the prime minister who is seen to be "one of the key perpetrators in this conflict".[84] Thus, from the onset the Democrat-led government's move to establish the Commission was regarded as an insincere gesture. Moreover, it has been noted that the government's continued imposition of the Emergency Decree has allowed it to take repressive measures against whatever it chooses to label a threat to national security. More serious than it may seem, under the terms of the Emergency Decree, the military takes over from the police authority as the primary agency responsible for security and thus holds the power to take control of any situation. In such a climate of intimidation, many doubt that an independent investigation can actually take place.[85]

Discussions: Diagnosis-Prognosis-Therapy Triangle

The previous sections of this chapter have attempted to outline the general context of the Thai security sector so as to illustrate that Thailand's SSG has long been defined by the overarching power structure of the Thai state. The Thai Southern conflict, as Kraft notes, "continues to take up state resources that could be used to address welfare and development concerns".[86] In contrast, Pongsudhirak views the political conflict of 2010 as illustrative of Thailand's overriding threats which are "fundamentally internal" – and short of a way out, there are bound to be "far-reaching consequences for security-related policy areas".[87]

Such overriding threats, deemed fundamentally internal, have been described through the Red Shirts movement in terms of the political power structure, which underpins Thai society.[88] In reply to the question of whether Thai society had been peaceful prior to the advent of the Red Shirts movement, Nethipo pointed out that it is fair to say that Thai society had been politically peaceful under democratic rule, but whether people were happy or not depended on where one's place in Thai society was. Peace is defined by the political power structure, which Nethipo explains by the metaphor of an entrenched triangle of power.

The first corner represents the power of the monarchy. Here, social ideology is dominated by state ideology where the monarch becomes effectively the centre of collective morale. Thus this corner is characterised by the ideology and symbolic attachment to the monarchy, which, involves the Thai identity: virtue, patriotism, nationalism, loyalty, Buddhism, etc.

The second corner represents the power of the aristocrats, the elites who have allocated their interests divisively. In effect, they are the high-level bureaucrats, politicians, the armed forces, businessmen, as well as the influential patrons.

Where then are the masses? Inevitably, they are within the third corner, which represents the power of the influential patrons' networks. This corner is thus characterised by informal networks of relationships, which cover practically everyone's relationship, whether rural, suburban, or urban, as well as a large number of those within the middle class. These networks bond the Thai population together in a hierarchy of powerful interests.

The three corners have bonded with one another and miraculously established a balance. In reference to the power of the monarchy, every social sector is under the influence of a homogenous Thai identity. The stability of the state's rule has been based on the establishment of the monarchy as the centre of collective morale. This stability has also tied into the various ideologies that together signify Thai identity: virtuousness, loyalty and peacefulness.

The aristocrats or elites, in contrast, have been able to divisively allocate their power based on their shared identity, which they also connect with the monarchy. As a consequence, Thai society has always lacked ideological differences. There was no need for ideological arguments, hence no fierce competition among political parties. From another perspective, the elites can also drive society and mobilise the Thai population in whichever way they deem fit, either as the influential patron, or through the networks of the virtuous, or those in important ruling positions. These elites are known to also include – besides politicians, bureaucrats and the armed forces – moral leaders, academics, and NGO leaders.

The influential patrons, or their networks, have perfectly co-existed with the elites due to their identical political tendencies, yet at the same time they are also firmly tied to the masses. These influential patrons share their interests with the elites, but they are elites in their own right at the same time. They are attached to the masses through their relationships, which may take the form of networks, old boys club, family ties, patron-client relations, or in the case of NGOs, a collective fight for a cause. Social movements are generally mobilised around issue-based demands, and the masses involved in the movements are part of the influential patron's network. For this reason, social movements have been limited within the bounds of the triangle of power and always ended up re-establishing the balance within the triangle, and thereby remained non-threatening to the structure that existed.

According to Nethipo, changes that have occurred in the past few years have disrupted the so-called 'political peacefulness'. For the first corner, the element of time and the insistence on maintaining the status quo by resistance to change has been the cause of instability. For the second corner, the elites can no longer agree on what constitutes their interests, due to the instability of the first corner. The elites once shared a single source of reference for the legitimacy of their power, but a rift has appeared among them, as completely different sources of legitimacy have emerged. The legitimacy linked to the strength of loyalty and Thai identity bestowed by the first corner, and the legitimacy that springs from the third corner are now both important and irreconcilable. The fact that these two sources of legitimacy cannot be reconciled has caused a major divide among the elites – a divide much deeper than that within the disempowered population.

The third corner has become an important factor in change as a result of the electoral dynamism that is now firmly rooted in Thailand. This dynamism began with the 1997 constitution, which allowed for the establishment of strong political parties. While some base their explanation on the Thaksin phenomena and the Thai Rak Thai Party, Nethipo instead focuses on the process of decentralisation initiated by the 1997 constitution as the critical factor that has brought election politics to the people's doorstep, in the form of policies that have an impact on the money in their pockets, health care, education and social status. This new dynamism within the system of election politics has led to changes in the distribution of political power that existed within this corner of influential patrons. There are two explanations for this.

First, the one-man one-vote rationale has resulted in the emancipation of once political subjects, transforming them into citizens and a source of legitimacy for state power. This has made it necessary for the influential patrons – political patrons, as well as powerful seniors whose power is based on the citizenry – to adapt and change accordingly.

Second, the electoral system, which emerged at every level, has formalised the powers of the influential patrons. Upon entering the local electoral system they have become visible, tangible, subject to choice, and can be weeded out. Citizens with the right to vote have come to realise that they can now negotiate their power with the influential patrons every four years.

Besides these changes occurring within the third corner, the power of the aristocracy has also changed – that is, they must now recognise the importance of the citizenry, and the votes that have brought them to political power, as the source of their legitimacy, hence the friction and conflict within the second corner as discussed earlier.

Nethipo concludes that the conflict presently witnessed in Thai society is the manifestation of the first and second corners' refusal to adapt in the face of changes in the third corner. This has generated an imbalance within the triangle of power and has become the cause of radical resistance. What this will lead to, according to Nethipo, depends on many factors within this triangle of power. However, if the existence of elites, state ideology, and inequity are common to any society, her suggestion in order to return to a peaceful triangle would be to seek compromise by way of political development through elections. This would mean that society's ultimate source of legitimacy would lay with the citizens and their right to vote, with the implication that corners one and two would need to adjust and adapt to find their place in a democratic society.

Both McCargo's argument regarding the Thai Southern conflict, and Nethipo's argument regarding the Red Shirts movement and the 2010 political crisis, point to the legitimacy challenges facing the present ruling power structure. McCargo contends that the Southern Thai conflict is a war over legitimacy – his point regarding the challenge to the legitimacy of the Chakri dynasty,[89] serves to explain the reoccurrence of violence since 2001 as the result of Thaksin's assault on the 'virtuous rule' and the 'network monarchy'.[90] However, it is important not to lose sight of the fact that the Southern conflict is in essence about the 'separatist' aspirations that have long challenged the legitimacy of the Thai state, and not the monarchy per se.

Similarly, Nethipo's explanation of the 2010 political crisis points to the changes occurring within the political power structure as the sources of legitimacy change. These changes challenge the legitimacy of the existing regime.

The preceding analysis of Thailand's political power structure reaffirms the observation that "the most important reforms in Thailand have been a consequence of much broader processes of social and political change".[91] In this respect, Beeson and Bellamy have argued that "simply applying an essentially Western framework to a non-Western environment"[92] creates certain discrepancies in introducing change to the security sector. While this could be partly overcome by "establishing the factors that influence security governance and change"[93], it is critical to have a "keen awareness of the historical forces"[94] that have shaped Thailand's security sector. For Beeson and Bellamy, certain aspects of Thailand's security sector reflect this point:

> Thailand provides a paradoxical example wherein it has engaged in perhaps more overt security sector reform than any of the states but without reforming the fundamentals of the way the military sees its role in relation to the monarch, the government and the people – a paradox that became only too evident in the coup.[95]

As such, the two ongoing conflicts aptly illustrate the context within which Thai SSG is defined and put to the test delivering security, especially now, at the stage of post-conflict peacebuilding.

Conclusion

The underlying predicament within the present Thai security sector is the two-fold nature of its crisis of legitimacy; i.e. – the legitimacy of the Thai state in the case of the Southern conflict and the legitimacy of the political system in the case of the 2010 political conflict. These two instances of diminished legitimacy have fuelled the political violence in the state's struggle to maintain its power and have also – and simultaneously – weakened the state's own authority. As a result, none of the political parties – not even those with the majority in parliament to form the present government – have achieved the widespread consent requisite to launching the necessary reforms that could restore a sense of faith on the part of the citizenry in the government.

The complexity of the 2010 political conflict notwithstanding, many see the conflict itself as a window of opportunity for political change. Optimistic as it may appear, the nationwide mass mobilisation and socio-political forces, which the conflict ignited, are raising demands for further democratisation and supporting calls for the reform of political institutions, including the security sector, as conditional to the reconciliation process.

Despite this, the question of reforming the security sector sufficiently to enable it to address this crisis of legitimacy – the source of instability and violence – is yet to be addressed and/or brought to any consensus among the contending forces. The current and unstable truce, as opposed to real political settlement, reflects the lack of consensus among all relevant actors regarding potential forms of resolution and/or mutually acceptable courses of action. The conditions that make reforms necessary have thus existed without the concurrent conditions required to see them realised, especially the reform of institutions closely tied to the security sector (the armed forces, the justice system, and the mechanisms which oversee state accountability and intervention regarding fundamental rights and civil liberties). Instead, in this quest for political legitimacy the monarchy has become more the target in the process.

The preceding analysis, that the current conflict situations have determined Thailand's prospects for and the (un)likely course of its SSR, is consistent with the view that the armed forces, in their various forms, as well as the institution of the monarchy have shaped the fundamental nature of Thailand's form of government. More importantly, this linkage has not only established the foundation for peace and prosperity within Thailand, but has also facilitated its system of democracy. As such, given the present polarised political climate, which put the armed forces and the monarchy on the defensive, as well as the dearth of expertise and inadequate effective power on the part of state and non-state oversight institutions, and the civilian government's propensity to politicise military control, Thailand's security sector under the present crisis of legitimacy is unlikely to see a prospect for reform in the immediate future.

Notes

1 M. Beeson and A.J. Bellamy, *Securing Southeast Asia: The politics of security sector reform* (Routledge: Oxford, 2008); M. Beeson, A.J. Bellamy, and B. Hughes, "Taming the tigers? Reforming the security sector in Southeast Asia", *The Pacific Review*, vol. 19, no. 4, 2006, pp. 449-472; and A.J. Bellamy, "Security Sector Reform: Prospects and Problems", *Global Change, Peace & Security*, vol. 15, no. 2, 2003, pp. 99-117.

2 Beeson and Bellamy, 2008, p. 104.

3 *Ibid.*

4 Interview, Chai-Anan Samudavanija, Committee on Reform Strategy, Bangkok, June 2010.

5 Beeson and Bellamy, 2008, p. 107.

6 *Ibid.*

7 Interview, Chai-Anan Samudavanija, Committee on Reform Strategy, Bangkok, June 2010.

8 Beeson and Bellamy, 2008, p. 109.

9 R.J. Muscat, *The fifth tiger: a study of Thai development policy* (Helsinki, Finland: United Nations University Press, 1994), pp. 139-142.

10 Beeson and Bellamy, 2008, p. 110.

11 Chai-Anan Samudavanija, Kusuma Snitwongse and Suchit Bunbongkarn, *From armed suppression to political offensive: Attitudinal transformation of Thai military officers since 1976* (Bangkok: Institute of Security and International Studies, Chulalongkorn University, 1990). The declaration was made under the Prime Ministerial order 66/2523.

12 S. Bamrungsuk, "Thailand: Military Professionalism at the Crossroads", in M. Alagappa (ed.), *Military Professionalism in Asia* (Honolulu: East-West Center, 2002), pp. 77-91. Revisions of such major laws included the Government Administration in a Crisis Situation Act of 1952, and the Martial Law Act of 1954. Also, the Internal Security Act of 1976 was abolished, and procedural changes in the use of the armed forces in riot control were also made, ending the Capital Peacekeeping Command, which had been a major instrument for controlling Bangkok's security since 1976.

13 Interview, General Boonsrang Niumpradit, Former Supreme Commander, Royal Thai Armed Force, Commander of the Peacekeeping Force of the United Nations Transitional Administration in East Timor (UNTAET) between 2000-2001, Bangkok, January 2010.

14 M.K. O'Conners, and K. Hewison, "Thailand's 'Good Coup': The Fall of Thaksin, the Military and Democracy", Special issue of *Journal of Contemporary Asia*, no. 38, no. 1, 2008, pp. 190-211.

15 Interview, Chai-Anan Samudavanija, Committee on Reform Strategy, Bangkok, June 2010.

16 Beeson and Bellamy, 2008, p. 111.

17 *Ibid.*

18 *Ibid.*

[19] *Ibid.*

[20] Interview, Chai-Anan Samudavanija, Committee on Reform Strategy, Bangkok, June 2010.

[21] Beeson and Bellamy, 2008, p. 108.

[22] These new institutions included the National Security Council (NSC) (a cross-institutional body), Accelerated Rural Development Agency (ARDA) and the Internal Security Operations Command (ISOC).

[23] Interview, Colonel Dr. Nares Wongsuwan, Director, Department of Research, Development and Graduate Studies, National Defence Studies Institute, Bangkok, June 2010.

[24] *Ibid.*

[25] There were seven cabinet changes during the time of the third National Social and Economic Development Plan (1972-1976) alone.

[26] In fact, Thailand clearly set out the relative responsibilities of the public and private sectors in its first five-year Development Plan (1961-1966). This meant that increased output was to be secured through private sector efforts, fostered and assisted by the government. The government's proper role was thus to not participate or enter directly into the production of commercial goods and services. Government priority in expenditure allocation was set clearly towards investment in economic infrastructure: water, electric power, and transportation. The military's role in this endeavour was clearly crucial for vulnerable rural areas.

[27] Muscat, 1994, pp. 181-182.

[28] H. Hänggi, "Making Sense of Security Sector Governance," in Heiner Hänggi and Theodor H. Winkler (eds.), *Challenges of Security Sector Governance* (Münster: LIT, 2003), p. 9. According to the definition of the security sector given by the Development Assistance Committee (DAC) of the Organisation for Economic Co-operation and Development (OECD), security governance refers to "the organisation and the management of the security sector". Thus the security sector would involve "all the bodies whose main responsibilities are the protection of the state and its constituent communities", the core structures of the security sector being, other than the armed forces, the police and intelligence agencies, the institutions that formulate, implement and oversee internal and external security policy, such as "judicial and penal institutions and elected and duly appointed civil authorities responsible for control and oversight, such as Parliament, the Executive, the Defence Ministry".

[29] H. Hänggi, "Conceptualising Security Sector Reform and Reconstruction," in Alan Bryden and Heiner Hänggi (eds), *Reform and Reconstruction of the Security Sector* (Münster: LIT, 2004), pp. 3-20. The four dimensions of security sector here comprise state and non-state security providers, and state and non-state oversight institutions.

[30] Bamrungsuk, 2002, pp. 88-89.

[31] *Ibid.*, p. 89.

[32] *Ibid.*

[33] *Ibid.*

34 Beeson and Bellamy, 2008, p. 124.

35 *Ibid.* Beeson and Bellamy contend that, "Military education remained largely the preserve of the military and the military command is only indirectly accountable to parliament. As a result, Thailand has only a handful of military experts in the civilian sector and – as in other countries where this is the case – most of them have been at some time co-opted into or by the government", p. 124.

36 *Ibid.*

37 *Ibid.*, p. 125.

38 *Ibid.*

39 *Ibid.*

40 Hänggi, 2003, p. 18.

41 A. Croissant, "Unrest in South Thailand: Contours, Causes, and Consequences Since 2001", *Contemporary Southeast Asia*, vol. 27, no. 1, 2005, pp. 21-43. According to official records of the total 1,975 violent incidents, which occurred during the period 1993 to 2004, 79 per cent took place from 2001 onwards. During 2004 alone, civilians and government officials killed numbered 573 and those injured numbered 424.

P. Chalk, "The Malay-Muslim Insurgency in Southern Thailand Understanding the Conflict's Evolving Dynamic", *Rand Counterinsurgency Study*, Paper 5 (Rand National Defense Research Institute, 2008). Between January 2004 and the end of August 2007, 2,566 deaths and 4,187 injuries were reported to have occurred, with civilians accounting for 70 per cent of all casualties. The form of attack, which has caused the highest number of casualties were drive-by shootings and assassinations: 3,253, with 711 police and 689 military casualties, while civilians accounted for 70 per cent of all casualties. p. 10.

42 D. McCargo, *Tearing Apart the Land: Islam and Legitimacy in Southern Thailand* (Singapore: NUS Press, 2009).

43 Chalk, 2008, p. 13.

44 *Ibid.*

45 *Ibid.*

46 Croissant, 2005, p. 21.

47 *Ibid.*

48 *Ibid.*

49 Interview, Former Ambassador Surapong Chayanam, Advisor to the Minister of Foreign Affairs, Bangkok, March 2010.

50 Chalk, 2008, p. 20.

51 *Ibid.*

52 McCargo, 2009, p. 9.

53 *Ibid.* This supporters network included Buddhist government officials and Fourth Army officers, most of whom supported the Democrat Party, along with a group of Muslim leaders.

54 *Ibid.*

[55] The Krue Se Siege which occurred on 28 April 2004 was an incident where 108 fighters were killed, 31 of whom were shot after seeking refuge in the central Krue Se mosque, one of the most revered Islamic religious sites in Southeast Asia. In the 25 October 2004 Takbai incident, seven months later, at least 78 people died in military detention after a mass protest at the Takbai police station in Narathiwat. It was reported that the crowd was fired on with live ammunition; some 1,300 demonstrators were subsequently rounded up and stacked in trucks up to five or six layers deep for transport to an RTA detention camp. By the time the vehicles arrived at their destination, 78 of the demonstrators had died of asphyxiation, and several dozen others had broken or dislocated limbs or were suffering from serious dehydration.

[56] The NRC was set up under former Prime Minister Anand Panyarachun.

[57] McCargo, 2009, p. 10.

[58] *Ibid.*, p. 8.

[59] Interview, Colonel Kongcheep Tantravanich, Operation Staff Officer, Directorate of Operation, Royal Thai Army, June 2010. See also: http://politicalbase.in.th/index.php/centrefortheresolutionoftheemergencysituation.

[60] Erawan Bangkok Emergency Medical Service Center.

[61] *ALIRAN*, "Thai crisis: Group appeal for non-violent resolution", 27 April 2010, n.a., http://aliran.com/1196.html.

[62] The peaceful roadmap comprised five points towards national reconciliation: upholding the monarchy, resolving fundamental problems of social injustice, enabling the media to operate constructively, establishing facts about violent incidents, and establishing mutually acceptable political rules.

[63] Protest leaders were concerned to seek guarantee of a fair trial as some faced charges for breaching state-of-emergency restrictions, while others faced terrorism charges, which carry a maximum penalty of death.

[64] Emergency Medical Institute of Thailand, 24 May 2010, http://www.niems.go.th/userfiles/12_24May2010_8AM.pdf

[65] *Associated Press (AP)*, 18 May 2010, http://www.guardian.co.uk/news/blog/2010/may/19/thailand-crackdown-redshirts.

[66] H. Hänggi, "Approaching Peacebuilding from a Security Governance Perspective", in Alan Bryden and Heiner Hänggi (eds), *Security Governance in Post-Conflict Peacebuilding* (Münster: LIT, 2005), pp. 3-19. As the incidence of internal wars and the phenomenon of failed states became more prevalent, it came to be recognised among the international donor community that the goal of security should no longer be confined to the state, but should extend to individuals and collectivities.

[67] *Ibid.*

[68] D. McCargo, "Thailand's National Reconciliation Commission: a flawed response to the Southern Conflict", *Global Change, Peace & Security*, vol. 22, no. 1, 2010, pp. 75-91. The NRC, headed by former prime minister Anand Panyarachun, comprised 50 members: 17 from civil society in the area which included Islamic council presidents, Muslim scholars, and academics, 12 from

civil society outside the area which included several prominent figures linked to the Bangkok NGO community, 7 from the political sector, and 12 from civil service and security forces.

69 *Ibid.* Tasked to investigate the upsurge of violence and to make policy recommendations to the government, the NRC between 8 April 2005 and 3 April 2006 held altogether 28 main meetings, four being in the Southern provinces.

70 McCargo, 2010, p. 77.

71 McCargo, 2009, p. 10.

72 McCargo, 2010, p. 89.

73 *Ibid.*

74 *Ibid.*

75 *Ibid.*

76 *Ibid.*

77 *Ibid.* McCargo noted that this was the view of "most members of the NRC, along with a narrow circle of academics, journalists and activists", p. 86.

78 *Ibid.*

79 The Committee on Reform Strategy is chaired by former Prime Minister Anand Panyarachun.

80 The Committee on Reform Assembly is chaired by M.D. Prawase Wasi.

81 To ensure their independence, committee members in each committee are selected by the chairperson of each committee and the government's involvement is limited to staffing and funding as necessary.

82 Other necessary reforms that have been called for involve the "resources and environmental management system, taxation and fiscal system, economic system, education system, justice system, political and state administration system, communication system, and others with a view to improving people's well-being, and strengthening and bringing fairness to society".

83 The Truth and Reconciliation Commission is chaired by Kanit Na Nakorn, a former Attorney General.

84 P. Lawansiri, "Thai Fact-finding Committee Falls Short", in *Irrawaddy*, 28 June 2010, http://irrawaddy.org/opinion_story.php?art_id=18817.

85 *Ibid.* According to Lawansiri "If the government does not want to change the trends of its methods, which have been roundly criticized as being insincere, and allow a truly independent fact finding committee that is acceptable to all sides, it must know that this process of national reconciliation will be labelled a failure and could lead to more mass protests".

86 H.J.S. Kraft, *Human Rights in Southeast Asia: The Search for Regional Norms*. East-West Center Washington Working Papers No. 4, July 2005. pp. 18-19.

87 T. Pongsudhirak, *Thailand's Security Outlook: External Trends and Internal Crisis* (Thai World Affairs Centre, Institute of Asian Studies, Chulalongkorn University, 2010), p. 1.

88 V. Nethipo, "The Structural Context of the Red Shirt Movement", paper presented at Thammasat University, Bangkok, Thailand, 2010 (in Thai), pp. 1-7.

89 McCargo, 2009.

[90] *Ibid.*, p. 8.

[91] T. Huxley, *Reforming Southeast Asia's security sectors*, Centre for Defence Studies, King's College, University of London, The Conflict, Security and Development Group, Working Papers, April 2001, p. 7.

[92] *Ibid.*, pp. 10-11.

[93] *Ibid.*, p. 10.

[94] *Ibid.*, p. 11.

[95] *Ibid.*

Part II:

Post-Conflict State-Building

4 Understanding the Security Sector of Nepal: Challenges and Prospects for Reform

SHIVA HARI DAHAL

This chapter looks at the case of Nepal; a country sandwiched between the two nuclear powers of the world, China and India. Nepal has remained as a choice of destination for many foreign adventurers to explore ancient cultures blended with the image of Himalayas. However, the country has been ruled by the absolute monarchy throughout its known political history until mid-2006 in one or another form, with an interval marked by the rule of Rana oligarchy for 104 years that ended in 1951 through a Revolution. Historical lead up events include the royal-military coup carried out by late King Mahendra Bir Bikram Shah in 1959 suspending the parliament and ending the multi-party competitive politics. Democratic politics was reintroduced in 1991 after the success of People's Uprising, but it suffers under extremely factionalised political parties coupled with frequent changes in government. A royal-military coup took place in February 2005 carried out by ex-King Gyanendra Bir Bikram Shah, but popular people's uprisings in April-May 2006 forced the King to step down from power, paving the way for restoration of dissolved parliament and the formation of an interim government followed by the formation of an interim parliament. The signing of the Comprehensive Peace Accord (CPA) in November 2006 between the Government of Nepal and the Communist Party of Nepal (CPN – Maoists); the promulgation of the Interim Constitution in 2007; and the signing of the 8-Point Agreement in 2008 between the Government of Nepal and the United Democratic Madhesi Front, an alliance of political parties from Terai-Madhesh, facilitated the task of holding election for the Constituent Assembly to draft a new constitution. The first sitting of the elected Constituent Assembly in May 2008 abolished the monarchy in Nepal and declared the country a republic.

The country is currently in transition from violence to democratic politics, and negotiations are underway to design the state structures of the Federal Democratic Republic of Nepal in the process of writing the new constitution. Reviewing the current discourses on security, this chapter explains the challenges of, and prescribes strategies for, security sector governance (SSG) in Nepal against the country's historical background and in reference to the transitional phase, ongoing negotiations for peace and democracy, and the process of drafting the new constitution. The chapter discusses the relevance of SSG to conflict management amidst negotiations over future state structures and systems of governance inside the Constituent Assembly, and suggests strategies to mitigate the gap between politics and security. The analysis of the substance and process reflected in this chapter is drawn under the presumption that the country remains in a negotiation phase that aims to complete the transition to democratic politics. The discussion in this chapter also takes note of the fact that the concepts of security, democratic governance of the security sector and national security policy are new in the political discourse of Nepal. Given the dynamic nature of Nepalese politics, this chapter touches only upon political developments in Nepal until 31 December 2010.

SSG and Peacebuilding

SSG reflects a broader concept of security, as it not only covers the military aspect, which has remained predominant in the state-centric concept of security, but also highlights the importance of non-military security actors for maintaining security in society.[1] Essentially, the definition encompasses the human security concerns of ensuring the safety and security of social groups and individuals at large. The definition is further refined in relation to the discourse on security sector reform (SSR), which promotes SSG under the conditions of democratic control and civilian oversight of security institutions. A wide range of actors and institutions are involved in SSR, in which 'democratic governance' is the unifying factor in the process.[2] Internal and external actors, statutory and non-statutory security agencies, legislative and justice institutions, executive and civil society actors, and internal and external oversight institutions all play a role in the security sector. Thus, the process of reform involves a wide range of activities and the participation of external and internal actors with a focus on 'democratic governance'.

Findings from recent studies on good governance, human security, transformation of societies by peaceful means, and democratisation have been incorporated in the domain of security. [3] However, emerging discourses on SSG are challenged to "develop both effective civil oversight mechanisms and viable and affordable security organisations capable of providing security for the state and its citizens within the context of democratic governance".[4] A key element in the process of reform is to ensure effective democratic control and civilian oversight over the security institutions, in order to enhance their capability to deliver security as a preventive measure against violence, which is often the result of the state's failure to guarantee security to their citizens and maintain stability within their territories. The security sector has been a part of the problems that have triggered conflict, and, therefore, it must be considered as a part of the solution in the process of peacebuilding.[5] The security sector plays a central role in conflict and in post-conflict societies, where internal security is threatened by the presence of a security system developed during wartime – typical characteristics of such a system include politicised security institutions, a lack of democratic and civilian control of the armed forces, government and private groups that continue to hold large stocks of arms and ammunition, and questions of legitimacy levelled at the control of security agencies by the state.[6]

Studies of peace and security have highlighted the interconnectedness between the need for democratic governance of security sectors and the process of peacebuilding, primarily focusing on developing countries in post-conflict settings. Peacebuilding, by definition, encompasses a range of processes, approaches and stages essential for rebuilding fractured wartime relations and redesigning social and political structures to transform conflict peacefully.[7] The importance of these two processes is undoubtedly clear in the context of Nepal – a country at the moment negotiating peace and democracy through the process of writing a new constitution in the Constituent Assembly. The constitution of a nation is the supreme law of the land: it documents the people's struggle for dignity and freedom in the past, but it is also a dynamic legal document that must address people's aspirations in the present and must be able to resolve any sort of problem that may emerge in the future.[8] Reframing a constitution and/or drafting a new constitution has been instrumental either to ending violent conflicts, or legitimising the outcomes of peace processes and political settlements in many countries around the world. More than one hundred countries have adopted new constitutions since the 1970s and the process has often been instrumental in ending violent conflicts.[9] A new constitution-making process offers an opportunity for building and/or rebuilding the nation; an opportunity for making a fresh start and breaking the past; an opportunity for ending violent conflict; and an opportunity for national dialogue, reconciliation, and the consolidation of peace.[10]

Since the new constitution in Nepal is still in the making, the exact contours of the democratic governance of security in Nepal are still under negotiation. The Constituent Assembly of Nepal is discussing different political issues, including the democratic provisions to govern security institutions to be enshrined in the new constitution. The National Interests Protection Committee, one of the thematic committees in the Constituent Assembly of Nepal, has been tasked to look at the security provisions to be incorporated in the new constitution.[11] The Committee has suggested provisions and conditions on mobilisation of the Nepal Army, as well as the composition and functions of a Security and Defence Council. In addition, a sub-committee of the Constitutional Committee has also dealt with security issues, in particular looking at the provisions for declaring a state of emergency and conditions for mobilisation of the Nepal Army.[12] The Constitutional Committee is expected to take the recommendations from these committees into consideration while drafting the constitution. The new constitution is expected to address competing political interests on democratic control and oversight over the armed forces, thus establishing principles of democratic control and civilian oversight of the armed forces, which are to be enacted through specific security laws. The new constitution, as a product of negotiation between the competing political interests, ultimately legitimises the process and contents of peacebuilding. In the modern era, legitimacy over processes of building peace and democracy is derived from a constitution that frames a political order to be governed by laws and regulations, and ensures separation of powers and stands for the supremacy of law.

The peace agreements signed so far by the political actors in Nepal have agreed in principle to begin the process of crafting democratic governance and inclusive structures of the security sector.[13] On the one hand, the peace process in Nepal is confronted with the challenge of holding the armed forces under democratic and civilian control; while on the other hand, voices are assertively calling for greater inclusion of ethnic identities in the security structures. However, these agreements are so vague that anybody can interpret the negotiated documents in their existing form to suit their interests. The peace agreements are also too weak to define the process of reform in the security sector. The agreements have provisions, for instance, for the "democratisation of Nepal Army", "integration and rehabilitation of the People's Liberation Army (PLA)" and "inclusion in the armed forces", but do not define the meanings of these concepts generally or determine the process of how, where and when these processes might take place. At the time of writing this chapter, the vagueness of past peace agreements has become a stumbling block in the peace process in Nepal, in which the question of redesigning SSG has remained central to political discourse. The consequences of a poorly designed framework for SSR on the peace process are further elaborated in the following sections.

The Challenges in Negotiations

The Constituent Assembly of Nepal had two years to draft and promulgate the new constitution, which expired on 28 May 2010. The promulgation of a new constitution would have been a logical conclusion to the current negotiation process and would have finally laid the groundwork for peace and democracy in the nation. However, the Constituent Assembly has confronted a number of contentious issues from the inside and the outside that have prevented the promulgation of the new constitution on time. The tenure of the Constituent Assembly had to be extended by a year through a 3-point understanding. This understanding was signed during the night of 28 May 2010 in order to prevent the country from plunging into a constitutional void and to ensure the resolution of a political crisis that could have gone beyond resolution by political means. Although the tenure of the Constituent Assembly has been extended, the contentious issues that blocked the process of writing the new constitution have remained unresolved; in other words, the problems have been simply postponed. Formation of a consensus government is one of the contentious issues that is outside the remit of the Constituent Assembly, but that is a provision in the 3-point agreement that facilitated the extension of time of the Constituent Assembly. However, a report of an informal dialogue with senior politicians from major political parties organised by the National Peace Campaign states that participants have arrived at a convergent view that the contentious issues inside and outside the Constituent Assembly are interdependent and interlinked to each other, and that failure to address them simultaneously has blocked the process of writing the new constitution.[14]

Inside the Constituent Assembly, there are a couple of contentious issues awaiting tough negotiation between political interests, including: models of federalism, a system of governance, the electoral system, structures of the judiciary, and the right of self-determination. However, the contentious issues outside the realm of the Constituent Assembly have dominated the constitution-making process, as the report published by the National Peace Campaign elaborates.[15] Of the contentious issues outside the realm of the Constituent Assembly, the questions of security governance have dominated the political discourse at the moment, in particular the process of management of ex-combatants of the PLA and democratic control of the Nepal Army, both issues which were left ambiguous in the peace agreements. Firstly, a decision has yet to be reached regarding the future of the PLA – a military wing of the CPN (Maoists) – in spite of the provision in the peace agreements for their integration and rehabilitation. Secondly, a framework for democratic control of the Nepal Army and its inclusive structure still needs to be negotiated and sufficiently discussed to explore all possible options with a clear agenda, acknowledging the interests of the people. Thirdly, the definition of 'democratisation' of armed force needs to be clarified, and mechanisms to implement agreements on security matters need to be developed to deal with the past legacy of the Nepal Army. In the absence of a negotiated settlement on these issues, the presence of the PLA and the yet to be negotiated status of the 'legacy of the past' of the Nepal Army have promoted fear and encouraged an environment of mistrust among the key political actors. Therefore, major political actors have consistently positioned themselves such that the new constitution will not be promulgated unless these security issues are resolved in advance.

Peace agreements, ceasefire agreements and/or national security policy build up a foundation to begin the process of SSR, which determines the objectives of the armed forces and the phase-wise and time-bound strategies for structural changes. However, peace agreements poorly define the process of reform, and a national security policy is still lacking in Nepal, despite the fact that it has one of the longest serving armies in the South Asian context.[16] A national security policy has yet to be developed given the changing political context and the security sensitiveness of neighbouring countries.[17] There are references to a national security policy in some security laws and elsewhere, but the concept of national security has yet to be clearly elaborated. Considering the geopolitical location of the country, development of a national security policy requires consensus among the major political actors of the country, as well as tacit consent from neighbouring countries, and in the case of Nepal, in particular from India. India, which surrounds Nepal from three directions, has historically had a greater stake and influence in Nepalese politics than other neighbours, and therefore has demonstrated interests in security matters.[18] A better picture of the Nepal-India relationship is visible through the prism of the Indo-Nepal Treaty of Peace and Friendship of 1950, commonly known as the 1950 Treaty, which was signed on 31 July 1950, and established a strategic relationship between the two neighbours. Article 5 of the Treaty further defines the security relationship:

> Article 5: The Government of Nepal shall be free to import, from or through the territory of India, arms, ammunition or warlike material and equipment necessary for the security of Nepal. The procedure for giving effect to this arrangement shall be worked out by the two Governments acting in consultation.

The Treaty also ensures free movement of goods and people between the two nations and close collaboration and relationship on foreign affairs and defence matters. However, the Treaty has remained unpopular in many quarters, but particularly among the forces of the political left in Nepal, on the premise that it undermines the sovereignty of the country. Increasingly, the Treaty has become a subject of resentment in Nepal, on the grounds of a breach of sovereignty and the undesired influence of India on the internal affairs of Nepal that it perpetuates. Perhaps, considering the security dynamics in the region, Aniruddh Gautam, a renowned political analyst, suggests that it would be to the benefit of both countries – Nepal and India – to revisit or redefine Nepal-India relations engineered by the 1950 Treaty.[19] His arguments are basically drawn from the grounded reality that the context of the 1950 Treaty and Nepal's status as a republic are drastically different. In Nepal, the popular social and political consciousness is comparatively higher than it was at the time of the Treaty signing in 1950. Nevertheless, India retains significant influence in the everyday politics of Nepal, as well as in the process of building peace and writing the new constitution. S.D. Muni, a renowned political analyst in India, insists that India's security agenda supersedes other political agendas, as it has prioritised a regional security strategy for South Asia.[20] Under this assumption, one may draw an argument that the agendas of peace and democracy in Nepal are of less priority and importance for India. Certainly, a country like Nepal would be in a better position to develop a National Security Policy and framework for democratic SSG if the country can accommodate the security interests of neighbouring countries, India and China.

India's influence is even stronger on the Nepal Army, given the fact that there exists a strong relationship between the armies of the two nations, which have been further reinforced through training provided to the Nepal Army by India. The relation between the armies is highly valued with the traditional practice among the ruling elites of Nepal to honour the Chief of the Indian Army as a General of the Nepal Army. Internally, India is fighting an arc of Maoist insurgency in its homeland and has concerns that their strength might have been advanced due to their relations with the Unified Communist Party of Nepal (UCPN – Maoists).[21] Externally, India is concerned over China's growing interests in Nepal, increasing contact between Nepalese Maoists and China, and considers the Nepal Army as a last defence against the UCPN (Maoists). In addition, Indian policy-makers hold the perception that should the Maoists become stronger in Nepal, and increase their relations with China, it may pose a serious challenge to their internal security. The UCPN (Maoists) has denied any relations with the Communist Party of India (Maoists) since the former embraced democratic politics in 2006 by signing the Comprehensive Peace Agreement.[22] Yet the security concerns of India have, to a great extent, prevented any attempt at modernising and professionalising the Nepal Army, and have minimised the prospects for negotiating the future of the PLA, as the UCPN (Maoists) have heightened concerns for their security in the absence of a power balance with the management of the PLA. Thus, the India factor is seen as one of the stumbling blocks in the designing of democratic governance for the security sector in Nepal, although it is one of the critical components of the peacebuilding process. As a result, the maintenance of wartime security systems, both by the state and the UCPN (Maoists), has continued with increased financial costs in comparison to human development.

Security and Development

The concept of security has been redefined and broadened during the last two decades with the recognition that the security of people and states are interdependent. The emerging meaning of security focuses on people, whose daily lives are under threat in violent conflicts that undermine rule of law, decrease the level of participation in political processes and increase human rights violations. Not only the concept of security, but also the traditional definition of development, which emphasises liberal economic growth, is being challenged and redefined by the emerging concept of human development.[23] Recent studies are broadening the meaning of development, bridging the gap between security and development with the construct of human security, which was first conceptualised in the United Nations Development Programme (UNDP) Human Development Report (1994) and shifted the focus of security from a state-centric approach to one placing people at the centre of the definition of security. The construct of human security articulates the need for the protection, safety, and freedom of individuals from threats of direct or indirect violence that can endanger their well-being, which is also the objective of development.[24] Both schools of thought are people-centric, attempt to address physical and material concerns of people, respect human rights and dignity, and argue that inequality and poverty are the fundamental causes of individual vulnerability.

The status of security and development, as well as the practice of SSG in Nepal, needs to be discussed against the background of poverty and security expenditures that have challenged the thrust of human security. Nepal is considered to be one of the least developed countries and ranks in the higher measures of poverty in the development indicators published by different national and international institutions. According to a survey conducted by the Central Bureau of Statistic, the poverty level is at 31 per cent.[25] However, a recent study conducted for UNDP by Alkire and Santos at the University of Oxford shows an alarming picture of poverty in Nepal.[26] The study uses indicators of poverty which are based on the status of standard of living, sub-categorised under ten different themes, such as education and health, and claims that 64.7 per cent of Nepali people are poor. Unfortunately, the expenditures in these sectors are low in comparison to the budget allocation of the security sector. Financial statistics published by the Ministry of Finance show the following allocation of budgets to different ministries:

Table 1: Budget Allocation to Ministries (in per cent values) [27]

Ministries	2008/09	2009/10
Ministry of Education	16.56	16.30
Ministry of Health and Population	6.33	6.23
Ministry of Home Affairs	5.28	5.74
Ministry of Defence	5.20	5.45
Ministry of Water Resource	2.52	2.94
Ministry of Agriculture and Cooperatives	2.44	2.75

The table shows that the budget allocation for the Ministry of Defence is comparatively higher than the budget allocation for other ministries. Total security expenditures in the country are increasing every year to fund the new security action plans under the Ministry of Home Affairs intended to contain ethnic armed groups in the troubled areas of the eastern hills and Terai-Madhesh. Unfortunately, security operations are taking place without acknowledging and understanding the perceptions of the people living in the troubled areas.[28] The Government of Nepal seems determined to deal with the emerging armed conflict with violence, and unfortunately the root-causes that drive violence in the troubled regions are simply undetermined. Although, this statement does not mean to suggest that criminal gangs in troubled areas should be allowed to establish a safe heaven. In addition, some argue that the total expenditures on the army are not covered in the statistics shown in the report published by the Ministry of Finance. Even so, the data published by the Ministry of Finance can serve as a basis of comparison, showing that the budget allocated for the Ministry of Defence was 5.2 per cent in the fiscal year 2008/09, and increased to 5.45 per cent in the fiscal year 2009/10. How the budget is allocated, and whether checks and balances are maintained in expenditures, are indicators of the level of understanding of democratic governance of the security system, in addition to other concerns such as legal and constitutional provisions to ensure democratic control of the armed forces. Security and development also need to be looked at with reference to security of identity as one of the integral components of human needs. John Burton, one of the founding figures of the conflict resolution field, suggests human needs are essential factors for human development.[29] Burton's list of human needs includes, among others, identity that constructs meaning of life, and becomes a basic need for many groups, the denial of which may lead groups to resort to violence for protection of their identity. The relevance of this theory is higher in Nepal, as the population of the country is composed of many different ethnic identities that have coexisted in harmony in society until recently. In the aftermath of the restoration of democracy in 2006, these identities are in the process of transformation,[30] and emerging identity-based violence, motivated by the search for recognition and the quest for political participation, has posed a serious challenge to internal security and the national transition to democratic politics. Management of internal security usually remains a challenging task in a country in transition from violence to democratic politics, and Nepal is an alarming example of such a case. Although the state institutions have not completely failed in the country, managing internal security has gotten out of hand for the ruling elites in Kathmandu. In order to secure their identities, ethnic groups are demanding better protection of their rights under the new constitution, participation in politics, and inclusion in state structures. However, these movements are, to some extent, confronted with counter-strategies adopted by the Government of Nepal.

Oversight of Security Providers

This section reviews the security providers in Nepal and the existing oversight mechanisms. It begins by looking at the Nepal Army, which has remained under the reign of the monarchy since its establishment, and even after the political transformation of 1950 and 1990, continued to serve the interests of the monarchy.[31] It was only in 2006 that the Army Act transferred control of the Nepal Army from the monarch to the elected authority; in addition, the Interim Constitution of 2007 enshrined provisions for civilian oversight and control over the armed forces. Despite these legal and constitutional provisions, the institution of the Nepal Army never embraced the peace process and is functioning independently as a state within a state.[32] On the question of inclusion of identities in the security institution, the institution does not reflect Nepalese social structure more generally and has never initiated any reform; although the PLA, established by the Nepali Congress in 1950 to stage a revolution against monarchy, was partially integrated into the Nepal Army.[33] The size of the Nepal Army substantially increased during the time of armed conflict from 46,000 in 1996 to over 95,000 in 2009. The large size of the Nepal Army was justified in terms of fighting the insurgency of the UCPN (Maoists). According to the analysis of International Crisis Group, the Nepal Army is the second biggest in South Asia relative to population:[34]

Table 2: Comparison of Army Sizes and Country Populations

Country	Army Size	Country Population	Per cent Value
Nepal	95,753	29,500,000	0.32 per cent
India	1,100,000	1,015,000,000	0.10 per cent
Bangladesh	250,000	15,000,000	0.17 per cent
Pakistan	650,000	172,000,000	0.38 per cent

The second largest security force of the country is the Armed Police Force (APF), a standing paramilitary force which was created in 2001 amidst the armed conflict. Trained manpower was drawn from the Nepal Police and the-then Royal Nepal Army in the initial phase, as well as from new recruitment carried out by the APF itself. The total number of personnel at the APF is around 25,000. The Act states that the objective of creating the APF is: "To maintain peace and stability in the country by protecting the people's freedom, lives and property".[35] The APF was created, as some analysts argue, as an alternative to the Nepal Army since the army, as per the directive of the monarchy, was not supportive of the policies of the elected government. According to Article 6 (1) of the Act, the APF can be mobilised to fight against armed conflicts, armed insurgency and separatist activities, and to control terrorist activities. Whereas, civilian matters are managed by the Nepal Police, the security institution established by the Act of 1956 and tasked with ensuring the security of civilians and maintaining law and order internally. The preamble of the Act states: "Having deemed it necessary to reorganise the State Police and to develop it to be a capable instrument to preventing and investigating crimes and maintain law and order".[36] The current strength of the Nepal Police is around 56,000 and the institution is under the control of the Ministry of Home Affairs.

In addition to the security providing institutions of the state, there are a number of armed groups fighting in different parts of the country, particularly in the mid-hills and plains in the south bordering India. According to the Ministry of Home Affairs, 109 of such armed groups are currently operating in the country, though only 12 armed groups fall under the political categorisation.[37] Eight of these armed groups hold on-and-off dialogue with the Government of Nepal. Management of non-statutory forces, which are not regulated by the law, is a challenging task, as these groups are frequently engaged in violence. There are neither clear demarcations to classify non-statutory security forces in the country, nor laws to govern non-state security companies; although such private companies are operating in Kathmandu and elsewhere in the country.[38] Problems also lie in classifying non-state actors such as the PLA of the UCPN (Maoists). The PLA, as the armed wing of the-then CPN (Maoists), began its operation fighting against the Nepal Police, initially, and became capable of fighting against the Nepal Army after 2001.[39] After the CPA was signed, the PLA was put under the control of the Army Integration Special Committee, and its cadres were placed in different cantonments monitored by the United Nations Mission in Nepal (UNMIN) that departed from the country on 15 January 2011. The analysis in this chapter does not look at the development of the politics and peace process in Nepal after the departure of UNMIN in mid-January 2011.

In a democratic society, existing national laws and regulations, together with the constitution of the nation, regulate and provide oversight of the functioning of security agencies, guided by the principle of democratic governance.[40] Legal and constitutional frameworks that guide the functioning of security structures are, in principle, the basis for judging the level of democratic governance of the security sector in a country. In a democratic society, security agencies and actors behave and act under institutional frameworks as designed by legal provisions, which determine the mandate, roles and hierarchies of security agencies, as well as delegate roles and responsibility to specific actors.[41] These legal frameworks demarcate the boundary between civilian, security agencies and government through the allocation of power and functions to relevant actors. In a broader sense, legal frameworks are the means of interaction between these different actors and institutions. In order to understand the legal framework designed to govern the security structures in Nepal, a review of some of the existing legal provisions is discussed:

Constitutional Provisions on the Nepal Army:[42]

> **Article 144(3)**: The President shall, on the recommendation of the Council of Ministers, control, mobilise and manage the Nepal Army in accordance with law. The Council of Ministers shall, with political understanding and on suggestions of the concerned committee of the Legislature-Parliament, prepare and enforce a detailed action plan on the democratisation of the Nepal Army.
> **Article 145**: National Defence Council: (1) There shall be a National Defence Council of Nepal for making recommendation to the Council of Ministers on the mobilisation, operation and use of the Nepal Army ...

Legal Provisions on the APF:[43]

> **Armed Police Act, Section 4**: The Government of Nepal shall have the power to inspect, control and direct the armed police.

Legal Provisions on the Police Force:[44]

> **Police Act, Section 4**: Powers of His Majesty's Government: The Power to supervise, control and issue directives to the police force shall be vested in His Majesty's Government, and it shall be the duty of every police employee to comply with the orders and directives of His Majesty's Government.

The legal provisions on civilian oversight and democratic control of the Police Force and the APF are comparatively clearer than the provisions on the Nepal Army. In general, the existing security laws in Nepal are so old – in some instances dating back to 1950 and 1960 –

that they are not compatible with the universally accepted norms of human rights.[45] Some of the security laws were enacted in order to support the system governed by the absolute monarchy and to uphold the feudal social structures. In the changed political context, public awareness is growing that the existing security laws are not capable of ensuring democratic oversight of security agencies, which have come under criticism for being ineffective in delivering security to the people, for being highly politicised, and for a lack of transparency in financial management. Once a government change occurs, which has happened frequently in Nepal over the last two decades, the general trend is to bring changes to the structures of the Nepal Police and APF according to prevailing political interests. Concerning the Nepal Army, the legal provisions and principles are so ambiguous, that they have led to contradictory arguments about whether the institution is in fact under the control of the president, the national defence council or the council of ministers.[46] In practice, there are competing arguments whether the Nepal Army obeys the orders of the elected authority – however, the resignation of two elected prime ministers in 2001 and 2009 over the contentious issue of mobilising or controlling the Nepal Army supports the argument that the institution is not under civilian control.

In spite of existing legal provisions, the oversight of the state's security agencies by government institutions is one of the weak areas of governance in Nepal. Allegations are rampant over the functioning of security agencies in terms of transparency in financial and human resources management, although the Office of the Auditor General has authority to audit the accounts of security agencies. The lack of clear legal provisions to judge the relative performance of security personnel is a contributing factor.[47] Yet, the parliament has the authority to control and oversee the functioning of the security agencies through its specific committees.[48] The Special Committee on Security of the Parliament can recommend policies on security matters, although its primary task focuses on the matter of states of emergency. The State Affairs Committee of the Parliament has a specific mandate enshrined in the regulation[49] and in the Interim Constitution to oversee security providers and relevant institutions. The Committee is empowered to control, regulate and direct the functioning of the security institutions, as well as to make recommendations for required amendments in the security laws. Moreover, the

Committee is tasked with the responsibility of making recommendations on the process and substance of the 'democratisation of the Nepal Army' as per the constitutional provisions.

One of the most criticised domains in the functioning of both state and non-state security providers is the legacy of human rights abuses committed by security forces during the time of armed conflict and the continuation of such abuses even after the signing of the cease-fire and CPA.[50] While the engagement of civil society in oversight of security providers is a recent phenomenon in Nepal, national and international human rights institutions have been vocal in exposing the atrocities committed by security personnel. International institutions like International Crisis Group, Amnesty International and Human Rights Watch have also called on the Government of Nepal to prosecute those responsible for human rights abuses, and are also seriously concerned over the continued impunity for perpetrators of human rights violations. A general problem in dealing with human rights abuses committed by the non-state security forces is that they are not bound by national and international laws in the same way as state security providers. The Nepal Army has a different arrangement – the allegations of human rights violations committed by army personnel are judged by the Military Court, although its procedures are neither just nor transparent.[51] This is one of the critical areas to be reviewed and dealt with properly in the constitution-making process: provisions must be built into the new constitution to bring allegations of human rights violations by the army into civilian courts.

Conclusion

Nepal continues to be in transition from violence to democratic politics and thus finds itself at cross-roads in defining the meaning of security as the capability of providing security for the state and citizens. However, these efforts are challenged by competing political interests and the concerns of regional neighbours. These relationships between neighbours need to be revisited in light of the considerable changes in social and political consciousness internally. Although the political leadership has demonstrated interest, as reflected in the peace agreements provisions for changes in SSG, the process of negotiations is suffering from a lack of guiding principles capable of facilitating interactions between security and politics. Preferably, a well-designed national security policy would have bridged this gap and facilitated negotiation on security matters. A national security policy can define national security interests and identify internal and external threats, if designed on the basis of consensus among competing political interests and tacit consent from regional neighbours. In addition, such a policy can be instrumental in designing a framework for the broader reform of existing security institutions or the creation of new ones.

The future of state structure and system of governance are being negotiated inside the Constituent Assembly, guided by the principle of federalism and democratic republicanism. The country would require new laws to govern the state institutions, including the security agencies, in a federal set-up. However, the existing security laws, of which some are decades old, enacted during the time of monarchy and reinforced by the ruling elites as the armed conflict unfolded a few years ago, are in immediate need of amendment. The existing security laws maintain the security system established during wartime, and in some instances prevent justice for the victims of the conflict. The creation of a justice mechanism to look especially at the allegations of human rights violations during the armed conflict and the enactment of new or amended security laws cannot be delayed on any pretext, as they are necessary in order to establish democratic governance of the security sector, to deliver justice to the victims of armed conflict, to serve the people, and to enhance people's trust and confidence in the security system. In other words, it is necessary to assure the population that the security sector is working for the welfare and wellbeing of all citizens, of all identities.

Notes

1 H. Hänggi, "Making sense of security sector governance", in H. Hänggi and T. Winkler (eds.), *Challenges of security sector governance* (Münster: LIT, 2003), pp. 6-8.

2 N. Ball, "Dilemmas of Security Sector Reform", in C. McCartney, M. Fischer, and O. Wils (eds.), *Security Sector Reform: Potentials and Challenges for Conflict Transformation* (Berlin: Berghof Research Center for Constructive Conflict Management, 2004), pp. 45-51.

3 UNDP, *Human Development Report 1994* (New York: Oxford University Press 1994); and N. Ball, M. Brzoska, K. Kingma, and H. Wulf, *Voice and Accountability in the Security Sector* (Bonn, 2002).

4 Ball *et al.*, 2002, p. ii.

5 C. McCartney, M. Fischer, and O. Wils (eds.), *Security Sector Reform: Potentials and Challenges for Conflict Transformation* (Berlin: Berghof Research Center for Constructive Conflict Management, 2004), pp. 6-7.

6 E. Newman and A. Schnabel, "Introduction: Recovering from civil conflict", in E. Newman and A. Schnabel (eds.), *Recovering from Civil Conflict: Rreconciliation, Peace, and Development* (London: Frank Cass, 2002), p. 231.

7 J.P. Lederach, *Building Peace: Sustainable Reconciliation in Divided Societies* (Washington, D.C.: United States Institute of Peace Press, 1997), pp. 73–85.

8 B. Acharya, *Sambidhanshabha: prakriya ra anubhawharu* [Constituent Assembly: Lessons and Process] (Kathmandu: National Peace Campaign, 2006), pp. 3-11.

9 V. Hart, *Democratic Peace Making*, Special Report No. 107 (Washington, DC: United States Institute of Peace, 2003), p. 2.

10 Acharya, 2006, pp. 1-2.

11 Constituent Assembly's Committee for Preserving the National Interests Preliminary Concept Paper, 2066 (2010), p. 1, http://www.ccd.org.np/index.php?action=resources.

12 Constituent Assembly's Constitutional Committee Report Regarding the Concept Paper and Preliminary Draft, 2066 (2010), pp. 19-22, http://www.ccd.org.np/new/index.php?cipid=12.

13 S.H. Dahal, "Democratizing the Security Sector in Nepal: Lessons Learned and Challenges Ahead", in B. Sapkota (ed.), *The Nepali Security Sector: An Almanac* (European Union: Geneva Centre for the Democratic Control of Armed Forces and Centre for European Studies, 2009), p. 8.

14 National Peace Campaign (NPC), *Constituent Assembly of Nepal: Challenges Inside and Outside* (Kathmandu: National Peace Campaign, 2010), p. 4.

15 *Ibid.*

16 H. Phuyal, "Introduction", in H. Phuyal and M. Urscheler (eds.), *The Securit Sector Legislation of the Federal Republic of Nepal* (European Union: Geneva Centre for the Democratic Control of Armed Forces and Centre for European Studies, 2009), pp. 1-2.

17 N. Acharya, S. Giri, J. Khanal, D. Pradhan and P. Thapa, *Rajyako punasamrachana* [Restructuring of the State] (Kathmandu: National Peace Campaign, 2006), pp. 44-46.

18 International Crisis Group (ICG), *Nepal's Future: In Whose Hands?* (Kathmandu/ Brussels: ICG, 2009a), pp. 18-23.

19 A. Gautam, *Support to the parliamentary committees: seminar with the State Affairs Committee and their visits to the security providers* (Kathmandu: National Peace Campaign, 2011), p. 14.

20 S.D. Muni, *India's Foreign Policy: The Democracy Dimension: With Special Reference to Neighbours* (Delhi: Foundation Books, 2009), pp. 20-25.

21 After a merger with other communist factions, the CPN (Maoist) renamed itself as the UCPN (Maoist).

22 S. K. Baruah, "Prachanda against anti-Maoist ops", *Hindustan Times*, New Delhi, 2010, http://www.hindustantimes.com/News-Feed/newdelhi/Prachanda-against-anti-Maoist-ops/Article1-566679.aspx.

23 S. Alkire, *A Conceptual Framework for Human Security*, Centre for Research on Inequality, Human Security and Ethnicity (CRSE), Working Paper 2 (London: University of Oxford, 2003), p. 37.

24 F. Stewart, *Development and Security* (London: University of Oxford, 2004), p. 2.

25 Central Bureau of Statistic (CBS), *Nepal Living Standards Survey, 1995/96 and 2003/04: Analysis of Panel Households*, 1st ed. (Kathmandu: His Majesty's Govt. of Nepal, National Planning Commission Secretariat, Central Bureau of Statistics, 2006), p. ii.

26 S. Alkire, and M. E. Santos, *Nepal Country Briefing* (Oxford: Oxford Poverty & Human Development Initiative, 2011), p. 1. http://www.ophi.org.uk/policy/multidimensional-poverty-index/mpi-country-briefings.

27 N. Acharya, "The Nepalese Army", in Sapkota (ed.), 2009, p. 128.

28 S. Giri, "State, Government and Security", in Sapkota (ed.), 2009, p. 105.

29 J. W. Burton, "Conflict resolution: the human dimension", *The International Journal of Peace Studies*, vo. 3, no. 1, 1998, http://www.gmu.edu/programs/icar/ijps/vol3_1/burton.htm.

30 L. Philipson, "A year of loktantra", *Himal South Asia*, vol. 20, 2007, p. 44.

31 Acharya, "The Nepalese Army", p. 128.

32 ICG 2009a, pp. 13-16.

33 Acharya, "The Nepalese Army", p. 128.

34 International Crisis Group (ICG), *Nepal's Flattering Peace Process* (Brussels: ICG, 2009b), p. 25.

35 Armed Police Force Act 2058, 2001, p. 1, http://nepalconflictreport.ohchr.org/files/docs/2001-08-22_legal_govt-of-nepal_eng.pdf.

36 Govinda Thapa, "The Nepal Police and the Armed Police Force", in Sapkota (ed.), 2009, pp. 157-158.

37 Nepalnews.com. (2009, September 7). Only 12 out of 110 armed groups political: Home Ministry. *Nepalnews.com.* June 21, 2013, http://www.nepalnews.com/home/index.php/news/2/1315-only-12-out-of-110-armed-groups-political-home-ministry.html.

38 A. KC, "Private Security Companies", in Sapkota (ed.), 2009, p. 229.

39 A. Dhakal, "The People's Liberation Army", in Sapkota (ed.), 2009, pp. 145-146.

40 H. Phuyal, "Justice Systems in Security Organizations of Nepal", in Sapkota (ed.), 2009, pp. 277-278.

41 B. Acharya, "The Nepalese Judicial System", in Sapkota (ed.), 2009, pp. 243-244.

42 The Interim Constitution of Nepal, 2063 (2007): eighth amendment. (Nepal Law Commission, Trans.). Kathmandu: Nepal Law Commission.

43 Armed Police Force Act 2058, p. 3.

44 H. Phuyal, *The Security Sector Legislation of the Federal Democratic Republic of Nepal* (European Union: Geneva Centre for the Democratic Control of Armed Forces and Centre for European Studies, 2009), p. 112.

45 Phuyal, "Justice Systems in Security Organizations of Nepal", p. 265.

[46] B. Acharya, *Setting Principles for Democratic Control over Armed Forces in the New Constitution*. Paper presented at the Seminar with the State Affairs Committee and their Visit to the Security Providers, December 10-13, 2010, Pokhara, p. 10.

[47] Phuyal, "Justice Systems in Security Organizations of Nepal", pp. 277-278.

[48] D. Sharma, "The Legislature-Parliament", in Sapkota (ed.), 2009, pp. 28-31.

[49] The Constituent Assembly (Conduct of Business of Legislature-Parliament) Rules, 2065 BS (2008).

[50] S. Pyakurel, "National Human Rights Commission", in Sapkota (ed.), 2009, p. 312.

[51] *Ibid.*, pp. 298-299.

5 *Trajectories of Security Sector Governance in Sri Lanka*

S.I. KEETHAPONCALAN

Due to the nature of the violence and its consequences, the ethnic dimensions of internal civil war between the Government of Sri Lanka and the Liberation Tigers of Tamil Eelam (LTTE) have been over-studied and several critical subjects of research value have been neglected. One of the neglected areas is the security sector in Sri Lanka. A lack of information in the public sphere, and a hesitation among those involved in military and security affairs to share their views in public, especially with researchers, as well as the security risks involved in studying the security sector, have deterred substantial analysis of this vital subject. Now the war has ended and Sri Lanka is seeking to transform into a peaceful society, and the security sector is likely to have a vital role to play in this intended transformation. In order to understand the role of the security sector in peacebuilding, a better understanding of the Sri Lankan security sector, the challenges it faced in the past, its current status, and the possibility of reform is imperative. This chapter, therefore, examines the trajectories of security sector governance (SSG) in Sri Lanka since independence in 1948.

As an emerging field of study, SSG lacks flexible tools of analysis; thus, in order to examine Sri Lankan SSG, this research develops its own analytical framework. Taking advantage of the framework, this chapter first identifies core SSG actors in Sri Lanka, before examining the pressure on the state emanating from 'secondary' security sector actors. The chapter argues that, as a consequence of the pressures exerted by these secondary actors, Sri Lankan SSG became dysfunctional. The pressures from secondary actors, however, have gradually dissipated. The most serious threat was removed, suddenly and rather unexpectedly, when the LTTE was eliminated in May 2009. Removal of the pressure will not automatically transform negative SSG into positive. Under these conditions a systematic and sustained programme is necessary to move the prevailing negative SSG towards a more positive footing. This would include, for instance, the enhancement of democratic governance of the security sector, right-sizing the armed forces, and making them more representative, as well as depoliticising the judiciary, strengthening human-rights protection mechanisms, and initiating a process of de-centralisation and democratisation.

Analytical Framework: Security Sector Actors

The security sector consists of "all organised groups in society that are capable of using force, as well as the institutions and actors that manage, direct, oversee and monitor them, and otherwise play a role in the development of a country's security policy and the provisions of its security".[1] Although this definition is comprehensive, the discourse on security sector actors also involves several different conceptions of the security sector.[2] The first rather narrow notion includes only legitimate legal actors: for instance, the Development Assistance Committee (DAC) of the Organisation for Economic Co-operation and Development (OECD) identified two broad categories of actors: the security forces and the relevant civilian oversight and control bodies. Among these, the OECD-DAC identified the following institutions as component actors in SSG: the armed forces, the police, and paramilitary forces, the intelligence services and similar bodies, judicial and penal institutions, parliament, the executive, and its dependent line ministries. This definition has been criticised as overly narrow because it focuses almost exclusively on state bodies. However, it is obvious that security sector policies and the capability of the relevant agencies, as well as the general culture of SSG, are all profoundly influenced by non-state security actors, including both armed actors and civil society movements.[3]

In contrast to this definition, the Human Development Report of the United Nations Development Programme (UNDP) identified five categories of security sector actors: (1) organisations authorised to use force (armed forces, police, paramilitary forces, gendarmeries, intelligence services, coast guards, border guards, custom authorities, reserve and local security units), (2) civil management and oversight bodies (president and prime minister, national security advisory bodies, legislature and legislative select committees, ministries of defence, internal affairs, and foreign affairs, customary and traditional authorities, financial management bodies, and civil society organisations), (3) justice and law enforcement institutions (judiciary, justice ministries, prisons, criminal investigation and prosecution services, human rights commissions, and ombudspersons, correctional services, customary and traditional justice systems), (4) non-statutory security forces (liberation armies, guerrilla armies, private bodyguard units, private security companies, and political party militias), and (5) non-statutory civil society groups (professional groups, the media, research organisations, advocacy organisations, non-governmental organisations, community groups).[4]

Especially in settings where the security sector is affected by internal civil wars and where neighbouring states are involved, regional security actors, not only the foreign armies but also intelligence and subversive elements, play a major role in the SSG of a particular state. For example, the Indian political leadership, intelligence agencies and the armed forces played a determinant role in SSG in Sri Lanka. Therefore, it is imperative also to take into account the role of external actors, especially military actors, for a better understanding of SSG.

Taking into account their different functions, influences, and impact, this chapter identifies two categories of security sector actors for analytical purposes: (1) core security actors, and (2) secondary security actors. Core security sector actors are entrusted with the responsibility of protecting the state and the population, most often by the political and constitutional norms of the system; whereas the secondary actors attempt to achieve their own goals by undermining or enhancing security. For instance, non-state armed groups may try to achieve a separate state, or greater regional autonomy by undermining national security and SSG. Civil society groups, in contrast, may try to achieve greater democratisation and good governance by enhancing SSG. International actors, mostly from the Western world, may strive to reform the system according to their own models through the instruments of loans and financial incentives. Regional actors, especially state actors, more often than not attempt to create a new security environment, which could enhance their own national and security interests by altering the existing security environment.

Core security actors include: (1) the organisations authorised to use force, such as the security bodies of the state, especially the army, navy, air force, police and intelligence agencies; (2) the executive, for instance, the president, prime minister, minister of defence, secretary of defence, and other relevant officials attached to the executive branch of the state; (3) the legislature, in so far as legislative bodies make laws and rules pertaining to the security of the state and population and oversee the role of executive in implementing security policy; and (4) human rights protection mechanisms, especially the courts, human rights commissions, ombudsman institutions, and similar institutions.

Table 1: Core and Secondary Security Sector Actors

Core Security Sector Actors	Secondary Security Sector Actors
Organisations authorised to use force: the security bodies of the state, especially the army, navy, air force, police and intelligence agencies.	**Non-statutory armed bodies**: such as revolutionary groups, liberation armies, political party militias, private security companies, etc.
Executive: president, prime minister, minister of defence, secretary of defence, and other relevant officials attached to the executive branch of the state.	**Civil society groups**: civil society organisations, media, think-tanks, universities, religious groups, grass-roots community groups etc.
Legislature: legislative bodies that make laws and rules pertaining to security of the state and population, and oversee the role of executive in implementing security policy.	**External actors**: foreign states (including armed forces, intelligence agencies, or subversive elements); international donor agencies and bilateral donors, international governmental and non-governmental organisations.
Human rights protection mechanisms: all levels of the judiciary, human rights commissions, ombudsmen, and other similar bodies.	

Secondary security sector actors include: (1) non-statutory armed groups, such as paramilitary groups, liberation armies, political party militias, and private security companies; (2) civil society groups, including non-governmental organisations, grass-roots community groups, research institutions and think-tanks, and religious groups; and (3) external actors, such as armed forces of foreign states and their intelligence agencies, or subversive military elements, but also other international interests, including donor agencies, and international governmental and non-governmental agencies.

Secondary security sector actors could be either reformist or parochial actors. Reformist secondary actors are the ones who try to democratise the system and ensure good governance by improving SSG: for instance, civil society organisations, international human rights agencies, and some bilateral and multi-lateral donors could be included in this category. Parochial actors are those seeking to achieve their own interests and objectives by undermining the democratic governance of a particular security sector. Obviously, guerrilla armed groups, liberation armies, neighbouring states that intervene in other states to achieve their own national and security interest, their intelligence agencies, and subversive units could be included in the category of parochial secondary actors.

This chapter argues that the level of pressure exercised by secondary security sector actors on the state or core actors shapes and ultimately determines the nature of SSG of a system. SSG may be categorised as either positive or negative. The higher the pressure from parochial secondary actors on the system, the more negative SSG becomes. The flip side of the argument is that if pressure from reformist secondary actors on the system increases, SSG may become positive.

An extension of this argument is that as the pressure from parochial secondary actors increases on a particular security sector, SSG will become more and more negative. Obviously, the system would try to remove the pressure by using different strategies. One of the strategies, which could be used, is political engagement and peace talks. If pressure is removed by peaceful means, SSG improves. In contrast, if pressure is removed through violence, then the transformation from negative governance to positive governance is likely to require a sustained programme, and the process could be protracted and cumbersome, as specific threats and threat-perceptions would continue to dominate the worldviews of core security sector actors.

Figure 1: Security Sector Actors

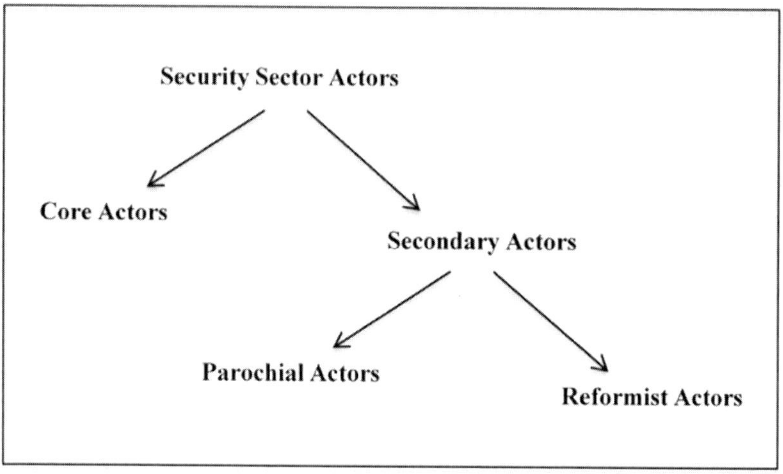

Figure 2: Security Sector Actors and SSG

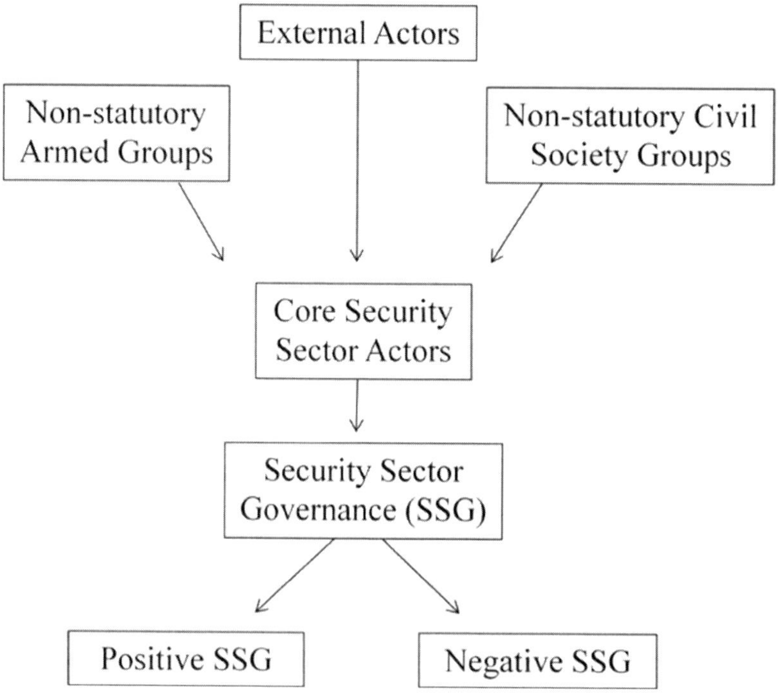

Table 2: Positive and Negative SSG

Positive SSG	Negative SSG
• Representative • Respect for rule of law • Superiority of the law • Promotes peace and social harmony • Respect for human rights • Strong civilian control of the military • Transparency • Accountable to the political leadership • Contributes to international peace	• Non-representative armed forces • Political authority above the law • Violates human rights • Weak civilian control • Lacks transparency • Weak accountability • Threatens regional and international peace

Negative SSG has less respect for the democratic norms, and violates the human rights of the population. It may depend heavily on nationalist rhetoric to justify human rights violations and anti-democratic tendencies. It also demonstrates weak civilian control, a lack of transparency, and a weak culture of accountability. It could also undermine regional and international peace. Positive SSG, though, reflects elements of good governance based on accountability, transparency, respect for rule of law, and human rights. It is representative of the population and allows for strong civilian control.

Figure 3: Relationship between pressure from parochial secondary sector actors and SSG

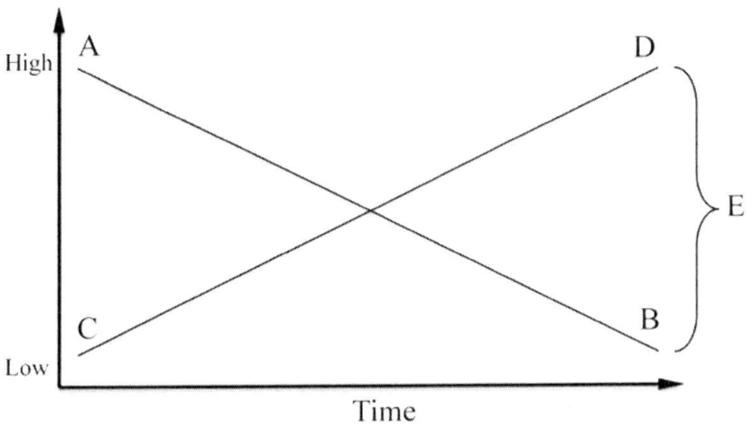

Figure 3 indicates the relations between the pressure from parochial secondary actors and SSG. Line AB is pressure from parochial secondary actors and line CD is governance. When the pressure is high (point A), governance is negative (point C), and when the pressure is low (point B), governance is positive (point D). Point E indicates the space where concerted efforts are needed to transform the negative governance into positive, if the pressure is removed violently and suddenly.

Core Security Sector Actors in Sri Lanka

The fundamental responsibility of securing and protecting the state and the population in Sri Lanka is entrusted to the following institutions: (1) the executive, (2) the legislature, (3) the armed forces, and (4) human rights protection mechanisms.

The Executive

After independence Sri Lanka adopted a Westminster-style system of parliamentary democracy, wherein the prime minister was required by the constitution to hold the ministerial portfolios of defence and foreign affairs.[5] This provision was removed when the first republican constitution was introduced in 1972. However, the then-Prime Minister, Sirimavo Bandaranaike, held these portfolios until 1977.[6] The United National Party (UNP) government that was elected to power by an overwhelming majority in 1977 launched an executive presidential system and introduced a new (second republican) constitution. Under the new constitution the president is "the Head of State, Head of the Executive and Government, and the Commander-in Chief-of the Armed Forces".[7] The constitution also confers on the president the power to "declare war and peace." Since 1978, presidents have also held the portfolio of defence, while at times having a deputy defence minister. Despite the presence of the deputy defence minister and the cabinet within the security policy-making apparatus, it is still the president who shapes all security policy decisions and controls their direction.[8]

There have only been a few occasions in which the president was not in control of the security sector. For instance, in 2002 the UNP government headed by Prime Minister Ranil Wickremesinghe signed a ceasefire agreement with the LTTE and initiated a peace process without the overt consent of President Chandrika Kumaratunga. The president later stated that she was not even consulted. This was one of the major security decisions taken in the recent past without the approval of the president.[9] Frustrated by the lack, or rather absence, of control over security matters, the president in 2003 brought the ministry of defence under her control and went one step further by dissolving the government, thereby proving that the president is in fact the ultimate authority in terms of security and security policy-making.[10]

With the coming to power of President Mahinda Rajapaksa, Sri Lanka witnessed an unofficial transfer of power, in relation to military affairs, to the secretary of defence. Earlier defence secretaries, like Austin Fernando, were civilian officials and did not possess much authority in security affairs. The present defence secretary, Gotabe Rajapaksa, is the younger brother of President Mahinda Rajapaksa, and is believed to wield extensive powers behind the scenes. One could, however, argue that, although the defence secretary regulates the day-to-day affairs and implementation of policy decisions, the overall control remains with the president.

The Legislature

In 1978, Sri Lanka adopted a combination presidential-parliamentary system as the new political framework. Therefore, the parliament, a unicameral chamber, is still a significant actor in SSG in Sri Lanka. Almost all security sector bodies have been legitimised by the legislation enacted by parliament: for instance, separate army, navy and air force acts provide the framework for operation of the armed forces. As an institution elected directly by the people, the legislature is in theory considered sovereign and expected to be independent. Parliaments of the 1978 constitution, however, almost always played a secondary role to the president, allowing him or her to dictate terms.

The Armed Forces

The third, but key component of SSG in Sri Lanka is the armed forces. The history of the armed forces began with the creation of the Ceylon Army in 1949 through parliamentary legislation.[11] At first a ceremonial force, the armed forces grew from mere thousands to approximately 200,000 men and women in the early 2000s. Today the Sri Lankan armed forces are comprised of a fully developed army, a sophisticated navy and a reasonably well equipped air force, in addition to a police force. The armed forces also include several affiliated bodies such as intelligence agencies, and possibly secret operations units, such as reconnaissance units.

Although the Sri Lankan armed forces are a powerful institution and very influential, they have, with only two exceptions, largely stayed out of politics and political issues. In 1962, a group of military and police officers planned a coup to overthrow the government of Prime Minister Sirimavo Bandaranaike. Since one of the conspirators, a police officer, on the eve of the coup, informed the government of the impending military scheme, the government moved in swiftly and arrested almost all the officers involved in the conspiracy. Many of them were sentenced to lengthy jail terms. It was clear that this failed attempt to overthrow an elected government was undertaken by a very small number of displeased officers without broad support within the military or the population. It was also not very well planned. In Pakistan and Bangladesh – two key members of the South Asian polity – the armed forces are more often tempted by political power and have staged several successful military coups. The fact that despite a problematic polity and social milieu, the Sri Lankan armed forces did not, or could not, take political power by extra-legal means has been depicted as an indication of the strength of the country's democratic tradition.

The other major incident, when the military intervened in political issues, occurred during the recent peace process.[12] As the ethnic conflict progressed and transformed into a civil war, the military began to occupy a large portion of the territory in Jaffna peninsula and other parts of the Northern Province, declaring them 'high security zones' (HSZs).[13] The gradual expansion of the HSZs created a humanitarian crisis within the Tamil community, as many families were forced to move to other areas as internally displaced people (IDPs). Demanding the reduction of the HSZs, the LTTE made the issue a precondition for further progress in the peace process in 2003. The military high command in the North, particularly the then-Major General Sarath Fonseka, who would later become a major political actor, openly opposed any move to alter the HSZs by writing directly to the media.[14] Except for these two major incidents, the Sri Lankan armed forces have remained under the control of the civilian leadership and take pride in this.

Human Rights Protection Mechanisms

In terms of human rights protection mechanisms Sri Lanka has three major institutions: (1) the judiciary, (2) the Human Rights Commission, and (3) the Office of the Ombudsman.

Rooted in the judicial administrative frameworks introduced by the colonial powers since the early 16th century, the Sri Lankan judiciary accommodates a relatively significant number of indigenous legal mechanisms, such as the *Kandyan* traditions, *Desavalamai* (a set of rules governing land and related issues in the Tamil areas), and Muslim laws recognised by the Muslim community in Sri Lanka. The Sri Lankan judicial system currently consists of a well-established institutional framework involving the Supreme Court, the Court of Appeal, the High Court, and lower level courts, such as the district courts, magistrate's courts and village courts. Traditionally, the system was considered independent and vibrant, and in fact it remained so in the immediate aftermath of the transition to independence. One of the fundamental reasons for the weakening of the independence of the courts in Sri Lanka is the post-colonial constitution-making process, which systematically eroded the power and capacity of the judiciary: for instance, the 1978 constitution conferred extensive powers over judicial appointments on the president.

The Human Rights Commission (HRC) of Sri Lanka was set up in 1997 in response to the growing concern over human rights violations in the country. Serious incidents of violence were reported throughout the country in the late 1980s and early 1990s due to the violent trends in the North, as well as in the South. It was believed that in addition to governments of the day, several groups were engaged in violent activities. In response to this trend, a democracy movement was born, resulting in the electoral victory of the People's Alliance in 1994. Its leader, Chandrika Kumaratunga, stood for democracy and human rights and won both the parliamentary and the presidential elections. Consequently, President Kumaratunga introduced a piece of legislation in parliament in 1996, which paved the way for the establishment of the HRC in 1997.[15] The HRC was conferred the powers to investigate complaints of alleged human rights violations by executive and administrative actions, review legal procedures, advise the government on human rights issues, and undertake human rights awareness activities.

The ombudsman is a government official who investigates complaints from citizens against the government or its functionaries. The official title of the office of the ombudsman in Sri Lanka is the Parliamentary Commissioner for Administration. Although established for the first time under the 1978 constitution, the ombudsman in Sri Lanka became prominent in the mid-1990s with the coming to power of the People's Alliance in 1994, as the new government revitalised the institution with new provisions, which enabled the people to directly approach the ombudsman with their complaints.

Pressure from Secondary Security Sector Actors in Sri Lanka

In Sri Lanka, the major pressure on the state stemmed from parochial (secondary) security sector actors, despite the fact that reformist actors were also active. Pressure from parochial actors emanated from three different sources: (1) the People's Freedom Front insurrection, (2) the Tamil insurgency and the separatist war, and (3) the Indian military intervention.

Except for the periodic anti-Tamil riots, Sri Lanka remained a relatively peaceful and largely democratic society until the early 1970s. In the mid-1960s, a group of Sinhala youth in the South, inspired by Marxist ideologies of socialism and revolution, mobilised themselves under the banner of People's Freedom Front (*Janatha Vimukthi Peramuna* – JVP). Rohana Wijeweera, the leader of the movement, was frustrated by the lack of revolutionary elements within the traditional leftist political entities in Sri Lanka. He advocated a violent revolution to cease state power. The movement and Wijeweera's ideas found resonance mostly among the university educated, unemployed, and rural Sinhala youth. As the movement expanded, the desire to stage a revolution also grew stronger. In April 1971, a hastily planned and poorly organised violent attack was unleashed against the state and its agencies, with the police becoming the primary target. This was the first organised attack on the security and integrity of the post-colonial Sri Lankan state. As a result, the state was unprepared to face the so-called revolution, but opted to reciprocate, meeting violence with violence.

The second major challenge to the integrity and supremacy of the state emerged from the North. If the JVP rebellion was inspired by socio-political factors, the northern insurgency was motivated largely by ethnic factors. The Sri Lankan Tamils, the major ethnic minority community in Sri Lanka, in protest of discrimination, demanded greater regional autonomy for the northern and eastern provinces, which they consider their traditional homeland. Three decades of non-violent struggle failed to force the government to concede political power, and eventually gave way to a violent campaign in the mid-1970s. Frustrated by lack of progress on the political front and the repressive tactics of the state, the Tamil youth resorted to arms and organised violence. In the mid-1980s, following the anti-Tamil riots of July 1983, the number of Tamil militant movements proliferated. In the early 1990s however, the LTTE emerged as the one and only Tamil armed group to fight the Sri Lankan state. The LTTE carried out an effective guerrilla campaign, combined with terrorist tactics, with the sole objective of setting up a separate state.

The third and most critical pressure arose from Indian interest and intervention in Sri Lanka. As the predominant power in South Asia, India traditionally assumed the role of 'security manager' of the region and considered South Asia in general, and Sri Lanka in particular, as its backyard. Also, Sri Lanka's geostrategic location close to its Southern border on the Indian Ocean makes the small state critical for the security and national interest of the Indian state. In the early days of independence from Britain, some Indian policy-makers believed that Sri Lanka should be annexed to the Indian state.[16] Therefore, India always had an interest in the affairs of Sri Lanka, and constantly monitored political developments in the country and its foreign policy trends. India preferred a friendly or neutral Sri Lanka. When the government of J.R. Jayewardene, which came to power in 1977, turned pro-West, the regional superpower was disappointed. Consequently, as a means to manage the government in Colombo, and to have a say in the affairs of the small state, India began to assist the Tamil militant movements. The task of propping up the Tamil militants was undertaken through Indian intelligence agencies, especially the Research and Analysis Wing (RAW) in Sri Lanka. Using the conflict as a pretence, India entered onto the scene as a peace mediator and facilitator. The Indian intervention in Sri Lanka culminated in the deployment of the Indian army as a peace-keeping force.

Some of the tactics India adopted in Sri Lanka, such as the delivery of food relief to war affected people in the North without the consent of the Sri Lankan government, and the eventual deployment of its military on Sri Lankan soil, had three major consequences in terms of the security sector environment in Sri Lanka. First, as the Indian army took control of territory in the North-East, the Sri Lankan forces were confined to their bases. It imparted the impression of a failed Sri Lankan army. Also, the Indian presence was considered by a majority of the Sinhala people as an infringement on their sovereignty, contributing to high level of hostility, socially and politically, towards India. A greater sense of tension and violence prevailed in Sri Lanka during the presence of the Indian forces. Second, the JVP made a comeback as a violent force, to stage its second rebellion based entirely on an anti-Indian stance. The JVP leadership argued that the government of the day was incapable of protecting the sovereignty and territorial integrity of the state against foreign aggression. The JVP unleashed a violent campaign against the state, especially the members of the armed forces and their families. Third, the Indian support extended to the Tamil militants made them formidable foes to the Sri Lankan armed forces. Although many of the Tamil armed groups welcomed direct Indian military intervention and deployment of the Indian Peace Keeping Force (IPKF), the LTTE consented only reluctantly and under duress. Hostilities between the IPKF and the LTTE broke out within a few months of the deployment. Indian armed forces entered the 'war' with the LTTE with high levels of confidence, believing that the rebels could be brought under control within a few days. The confrontation, however, continued for about two years, and India lost about one thousand men with several hundred injured. The level of violence that had prevailed in Sri Lanka was thus multiplied many fold with the introduction of the Indian forces.

Emergence of Negative SSG

In the immediate aftermath of independence, the Sri Lankan armed forces, especially the army, which was being built up rather slowly, was considered a ceremonial force.[17] More often than not it was called on to control riots and to protect the borders from illegal migrants from India. Except for one occasion where a small number of agitating protesters was shot and killed by the police during the 1953 *hartal* – a protest campaign organised by the leftist movement – excessive use of violence was never reported. In the early days of independence governments were also sensitive about the actions of the security forces. For example, in response to the killing of a few protesters by the police in 1953 and the emerging tense situation, Prime Minister Dudley Senanayake resigned from his position. Therefore, one could safely argue that Sri Lanka in this period demonstrated qualities of positive SSG.

However, with the pressure mounting from parochial secondary actors, a rapid transformation took place where all components of the security sector contributed to the emergence of a negative SSG. For instance, the armed forces expanded dramatically, became less representative and homogenous, engendered weak civilian control, were accused of serious human rights violations, and grew beyond the jurisdiction of civilian law. They also became politically ambitious. One of the most striking features of the Sri Lankan armed forces is its rapid expansion in terms of numbers since the early 1980s. Analysing the failed coup of 1962, Robert Kearny pointed out that Sri Lanka was cited as the most unlikely place in South Asia for a military coup, largely due to its small size and lack of distinguished military tradition.[18] In the early 1960s "the army numbered slightly more than 5,000, the navy under 2,000, and the air force a little more than 1,000 men. The police force of more than 9,000 men is larger than the combined military services".[19] Pavey and Smith point out that:

> [T]hroughout the 1990s, as internal security threats increased from both the LTTE in the north and east and the Marxist, nationalist JVP uprising in the south, the security forces increased rapidly in both size and capability, almost doubling in size between 1990 and 1996 to reach an expanded level of 95,000 for the last few years of the decade. Today, the Sri Lankan armed forces stand at over 200,000 military personnel.[20]

Despite the intensity of the security threat that emanated from the JVP and the LTTE, it was recognised that Sri Lanka had over-sized its armed forces.

As the size, capacity and value of the armed forces magnified, its political role and ambitions also increased. Although no major or known attempts were made to stage a military coup after 1962, the role and influence of the military personnel in politics certainly increased. In contrast to the early days of independence, several military leaders have entered active politics in the recent past. For instance, Major General Janaka Parera, a revered military hero of the South, contested the provincial council election in 2008 representing the main opposition party, the UNP.[21] General Sarath Fonseka, who led the army as its commander and provided leadership to the entire military campaign during the final war with the LTTE, entered politics even before he was completely discharged from active service. He contested the 2010 presidential election as the common candidate of the major opposition parties and posed a serious challenge to the incumbent president, who otherwise was extremely popular, having won the war against the LTTE. Immediately after the election, the government detained him on the claim that he was conspiring to overthrow the government with the help of deserted military officers. Eventually, he was sentenced to 30 months of imprisonment. General Fonseka certainly symbolised the growing influence of the military in politics.

The growing political clout of the military has also led to greater accommodation of military personnel by successive governments. A large number of former leaders of the armed forces have been appointed to civil service and the diplomatic corps, and have been brought into the state mechanism as chairmen, governors, commissioners etc. Rear Admiral (retired) Mohan Wijewickrama served as the governor of the Eastern Province; Major General G.A. Chandrasiri was appointed as the governor of the Northern Province in 2009; and the prison system is headed by Major General V.R. de Silva. Some military leaders have been sent abroad as ambassadors. For instance, former Air Force Commander and Chief of Staff Donald Perera is currently serving as the Sri Lankan ambassador to Israel. The present defence secretary, who commands substantial authority, also served in the military. It is possible that military personnel are accommodated in great numbers in order to mitigate the temptation to overthrow elected governments. Currently, civilian structures, for instance non-governmental organisations and urban development authorities, have been placed under the Ministry of Defence. Moreover, new university students are required to undergo what is called 'leadership training', provided by the military. Civilian control of the military is an essential aspect of good governance, but Sri Lanka seems to be moving in the opposite direction as increasing military control is introduced to civilian matters.

As the ethno-political conflict intensified and the state began to see the Tamils as enemies and potential terrorists, the armed forces, as an institution, failed to reflect the multi-ethnic characteristic of the society. The Sinhala-Buddhistisation of the armed forces was accelerated following the failed military coup of 1962 where almost all the conspirators came from religious or ethnic minorities. This factor motivated the rulers to exclude members of the minority communities, especially the Tamils, from the security services. In 1956, according to one account, about 40 per cent of the armed forces were Tamils.[22] The strength of the minority communities fell sharply in the 1970s and 1980s, and currently about 99 per cent of armed forces is Sinhalese, mostly Buddhists. The Tamil nationalists call the Sri Lankan armed forces the Sinhala Army.

Use of extreme force became synonymous with the armed forces in the post-1971 period. A large number of suspected insurgents were killed, and the armed forces demonstrated the capacity to employ unlimited force, if necessary, in 1971. In the late 1980s, when the JVP made a comeback as a more determined and violent force using terrorist tactics, the armed forces met the threat with equal force. The deployment of the IPKF enabled the government of the day to exert its full strength on the JVP. The LTTE also employed terrorist tactics and constantly used violence against civilian as well as military targets. The armed forces were also accused of intentionally using violence against civilian targets, as well as disproportionate force. During the final war, according to some international human rights observers, several thousand civilians were killed by the LTTE and the armed forces. The government, however, maintains that it followed a policy of zero civilian casualties, and that no Tamil civilians were killed by state forces.

As noted above, the executive, especially the office of the president, is the most critical political actor in SSG in Sri Lanka. Almost all fundamental decisions pertaining to the war and the security forces in the recent past have been determined by the president directly, despite the presence of other actors, such as the prime minister and cabinet. Neglecting the security forces or compromising their interests would be political suicide. Therefore, annual budget allocations for the security sector have increased gradually but steadily, while allocations for social welfare schemes, including health and education, have increasingly suffered.[23] Following the end of the war, it was expected that the security allocation for the year 2010 would be reduced and that other essential services would get more attention, having suffered heavily in the past due to the mounting cost of war. Yet, surprisingly, the defence budget was boosted by 26 billion rupees, and the total allocation for security sector in the 2010 budget – at 202 billion rupees – remained higher than the allocation for health, education and welfare schemes, combined.[24]

The contribution of the legislature to the emergence of negative SSG, and perhaps even the escalation of the conflict itself, cannot be underestimated. In the post-independence era, parliament remained a majoritarian institution and thus was easily able to enact laws prejudicing the interests of the minority communities. Parliament, however, enacted two particularly important pieces of legislation, which had far-reaching consequences for SSG: the Emergency Regulations (ER), and the Prevention of Terrorism Act (PTA). The ER legislation was enacted in response to the first JVP rebellion of 1971 and was subsequently altered on several occasions, conferring more and more powers to the armed forces. For a lengthy period the country was ruled under the ER because it provided successive governments with a strong grip on power, and an effective tool to counter opposition parties and the media. It was in response to the growing threat from the Tamil militants, and especially the LTTE, that the PTA was introduced in 1979. According to a 2009 report from the International Commission of Jurists:

> [T]he Sri Lankan legal system has rarely succeeded in holding perpetrators accountable for these violations. On the contrary, the complex and confusing emergency and anti-terrorism laws that have been put into place have frequently served to exasperate rather than resolve the crisis by infringing on the rights of ordinary citizens, including human rights defenders, lawyers and journalists.[25]

Critics often call the PTA 'draconian'.[26] Due to the severity and abusive nature of these pieces of legislation, successive governments were asked to repeal the ER and PTA. For example, in 1999, the United Nations Working Group on Enforced or Involuntary Disappearances recommended that the emergency regulations "should be abolished or otherwise brought into line with internationally accepted standards of personal liberty, due process of law and humane treatment of prisoners".[27]

The Sri Lankan legal system and the judiciary, although independent in theory, have come under severe criticism for corruption, politicisation, and inefficiency. Analysts describe the system as dysfunctional and see it as a reason for Sri Lanka attaining the status of a "failed state".[28] The courts in general have become ethno-centric, as they have failed to protect the rights of the minority communities. Suspected LTTE members have been detained without trial for years. There were complaints that the courts issue disproportionately severe punishments to suspects from minority communities. Also, the International Crisis Group (ICG) claimed that:

> Rather than assuaging conflict, Sri Lanka's courts have corroded the rule of law and worsened ethnic tensions. Rather than constraining militarisation and protecting minority rights, a politicised bench has entrenched favoured allies, punished foes and blocked compromises with the Tamil minority.[29]

At the same time, two prominent human rights protection mechanisms – the ombudsman and the HRC – have become dysfunctional and futile. The HRC suffers from lack of will and inadequate resources to fulfil its responsibilities. No core security sector actors, including the members of the HRC, wanted to risk undermining security operations against the LTTE. It was feared that a vibrant human rights agenda would go against the goal of eliminating 'terrorism'. Therefore, the HRC was allowed to dwindle through the appointment of weak and politically biased personalities to the leadership of the organisation, and a lack of adequate resources also hampered its operations. This was also true of the ombudsman.

The Removal of Pressure

The combined effect of the policies and actions of the core security sector actors and the parochial secondary actors in Sri Lanka led to the emergence of negative SSG. The pressures from parochial actors, however, were systematically and efficiently removed. With the assistance of friendly states, the Sri Lankan government pitted its under-prepared and semi-built armed forces against the JVP in 1971, ultimately bringing the rebellion under control. Hard-core members of the movement were sentenced to various jail terms: for instance, the leader of the rebels, Rohana Wijeweera, was sentenced to 20 years imprisonment. With the 1989 assassination of almost all the members of the JVP central committee – the only exception being the current leader, Somawansa Amarasinghe – the second rebellion was effectively terminated. Thousands of actual or suspected JVP cadres were killed in this campaign. In the mid-1990s, the JVP transformed itself into a political party and currently practices radical, but democratic, politics.

Pressure from the regional superpower, India, was also removed through collaboration between the LTTE and the Government of Sri Lanka, headed by President Premadasa. Premadasa was elected to power in 1989 and quickly demanded the withdrawal of the IPKF, claiming openly that the presence of IPKF in the country was a violation of Sri Lanka's sovereignty. This position brought the LTTE, which was already fighting the IPKF, and the Government of Sri Lanka together, and they worked in collaboration with the common goal of ousting the IPKF. Consequently, India withdrew its forces from Sri Lanka in 1990. The withdrawal of the IPKF, and the improved ties between India and Sri Lanka, eased the pressure from India. However, the LTTE evolved into a more determined and sophisticated force and continued its violent campaign to create a separate state. Attempts to resolve the conflict politically did not succeed, as both parties lacked the will to compromise. This led to a fresh round of confrontations. President Mahinda Rajapaksa, who carried out a determined campaign against the LTTE with the able assistance from friendly states like India, China and Pakistan, eventually oversaw the comprehensive defeat of the rebels. In May 2009, the LTTE leadership, including its chief Velupillai Prapakaran, was killed and more than 10,000 cadres surrendered to the armed forces. The comprehensive defeat of the LTTE has to a great extent removed the pressure from parochial secondary actors on the state.

In Sri Lanka pressure also derives from reformist secondary security sector actors, especially from local civil society organisations and donors. Civil society has always been vibrant and involved heavily in peacebuilding and good governance-related issues. Donors, particularly Western bilateral donors, insist on improvement of governance, peacebuilding and human rights programmes, and impose a sort of conditionality on monetary assistance. Western multi-lateral donors also encourage good governance: for instance, the European Union was heavily involved in the recent peace process and extended a preferential trade agreement to Sri Lanka (the Generalised System of Preferences Plus facility), which demands compliance with international legal and human rights standards. However, pressure from reformist actors, in relation to parochial actors, was extremely weak and had hardly any capacity to alter security policies or attitudes. For instance, the substantial financial assistance extended to Sri Lanka at the Tokyo Donor Conference of 2003 failed to lead the country to peace and to prevent the recurrence of war.

Conclusion

The major pressure on the state from a parochial secondary security sector actor, the LTTE, was removed suddenly, and rather unexpectedly, in 2009. This sudden removal of pressure did not automatically shift prevailing negative SSG onto a more positive footing, as threats and threat perceptions still continue to dominate the thinking of core actors. A sustained and coordinated programme is needed to shift from negative to positive SSG. This process could be cumbersome and slow. The programme should entail several elements, and primary among them must be an SSR process. However, the concept of SSR has been understood in Sri Lanka as an essentially Western idea, and a process aimed at weakening the power of the security forces. At least partly due to this attitude, the only reform initiative introduced during the last peace process failed. Alternative terms, such as democratic enhancement of the security forces, may be more acceptable than SSR in Sri Lanka. As indicated already, the Sri Lankan armed forces are over-sized and spend too much. It is therefore imperative to decrease the armed forces to the right size and to gradually reduce defence expenditures to align with real needs. The annual budget should balance defence expenditures with other necessary expenditures for social development. Since the current composition of the armed forces is not ethnically representative, any new recruitment scheme should focus on minority communities. Depoliticising the judiciary and encouraging an independent judicial culture is essential. Strengthening the HRC and the ombudsman would certainly reinforce the human security aspect of Sri Lanka's security culture. The security sector in Sri Lanka suffers from excessive centralisation of political power. Therefore, a process of decentralisation and democratisation would speed up the transformation from negative to positive SSG.

Notes

1 DCAF, *Security Sector Governance and Reform*, DCAF Backgrounder 05/2009 (Geneva: Geneva Centre for the Democratic Control of Armed Forces, 2009), p. 2.

2 For a brief discussion on this subject see H. Hänggi, "Making Sense of Security Sector Governance", in H. Hänggi and T. Winkler (eds.), *Challenges of Security Sector Governance* (Münster: LIT, 2003), pp. 3-22.

3 DAC Task Force on Conflict, *Peace and Development Co-operation, Security Issues and Development Co-operation: A Conceptual Framework for Enhancing Policy Coherence* (Paris: Organisation for Economic Co-operation and Development, 2000).

4 UNDP, *Human Development Report 2002: Deepening Democracy in a Fragmented World* (New York: Oxford University Press), p. 87.

5 Section 46 (4) of the Soulbury (independence) Constitution.

6 See: Shelton Kodikara, *Foreign Policy of Sri Lanka* (Delhi: Chanakya Publications, 1992), p. 4.

7 Article 30 (1) of the Constitution of the Democratic Socialist Republic of Sri Lanka, 1978.

8 All major policy decisions of the government need to be endorsed by the cabinet.

9 Austin Fernando, *My Belly is White* (Colombo: Vijitha Yapa Publishers, 2008), p. 925.

10 S.I. Keethaponcalan, *Sri Lanka: Politics of Power, Crisis and Peace, 2002- 2005* (Colombo & Chennai: Kumaran Book House, 2009), p. 135.

11 Army Act No. 17 of 1949.

12 This peace process was undertaken between the Government of Sri Lanka and the LTTE from 2002-04.

13 The Northern Province was the locus of the military confrontation between the armed forces of the state and the LTTE. Jaffna is the major city in the Northern Province and it was the center of Tamil culture and politics. It is here the LTTE initially started its activities as a small-armed group.

14 See Keethaponcalan, 2009, pp. 103-05.

15 The Human Rights Commission Act No 21 of 1996.

16 Shelton Kodikara, *Foreign Policy of Sri Lanka* (Delhi: Chanakya Publications, 1992).

17 Eleanor Pavey and Chris Smith, "Post-Conflict Reconstruction and Security Sector Reform in Sri Lanka", in Hans Born and Albrecht Schnabel (eds.), *Security Sector Reform in Challenging Environments* (Munster, ILT, 2009), pp. 189-210.

18 Robert N. Kearney, "The New Political Crisis of Ceylon", *Asian Survey*, vol. 2, no. 4, 1962, pp. 19-27.

19 *Ibid*, p. 26.

20 Pavey and Smith, 2009, p. 196.

21 He was killed by a suicide bomber during the election campaign.

22 Cited in Pavey and Smith, 2009. Also see, Cynthia Encloe, *Ethnic Soldiers: State Security in a Divided Society* (London: Penguin, 1980).

[23] For a detailed description of statistics, see Harry Goonetileke, "Counting the Cost of a Weary War", in Kumar Rupesinghe (ed.), *Negotiating Peace in Sri Lanka, Efforts, Failures, & Lessons* (London: International Alert, 1998), p. 341.

[24] Ashok Mehta, "Unfazed by Calumny", *The Pioneer*, 7 July 2010, https://groups.google.com/forum/?fromgroups#!topic/soc.culture.tamil/WWfy6Ml2cBw.

[25] International Commission of Jurists, *Sri Lanka: Briefing Paper. Emergency laws and International Standards*, March 2009, p. i.

[26] BBC News South Asia, "Human Rights Watch Condemn draconian Sri Lankan Law", September 11, 2011, http://www.bbc.co.uk/news/world-south-asia-1483 9493.

[27] Amnesty International, *Sri Lanka, New Emergency Regulations – Erosion of Human Rights Protection*, July 2000, p. 1.

[28] Jasmine Joseph, *Sri Lanka's Dysfunctional Criminal System* (Hong Kong: Asian Human Rights Commission, 2007), p. 5.

[29] International Crisis Group (ICG), *Sri Lanka's Judiciary: Politicized Courts, Compromised Rights* (Bangkok/Brussels: International Crisis Group, 2009), p. 1.

6 Peacebuilding and Security Sector Governance in Timor-Leste

NÉLSON BELO

Timor-Leste is a country whose independence was achieved through the efforts of its people, often times through violent actions in the cities, and combat in the forests and jungles of the Timorese countryside. Almost all Timorese people were involved one way or another in contributing to the struggle for independence. There is great respect for the veterans of the resistance, both the members of the Armed Forces for the National Liberation of Timor-Leste (*Forças Armadas da Libertação Nacional de Timor-Leste* – Falintil) and those of the clandestine front. Many people from these organisations have felt compelled to continue their contribution to their country and are involved in the security sector, serving either in the police, military, parliament, or civil society.

Security Sector Governance (SSG) is an important issue in Timor-Leste because of this history of struggle. The Timorese people did not receive much international governmental assistance or support during their struggle and therefore were forced to face the fact that they would not be able to achieve independence through negotiations and lobbying, but would instead have to fight for it. Groups were formed to oppose and resist the Indonesian occupation, and some of those groups are still in existence today, having not disbanded once independence was gained. Twenty-four years of violent struggle have affected society, especially the minds of the younger generations. Having witnessed the violence and many human rights violations committed by the Indonesian forces during the occupation, people tend to believe that violence is a normal everyday occurrence.

Because Timor-Leste is a young country and has a history of resistance, the Timorese must work hard to transform their young people and their resistance mentality into a force of positive change that will contribute to societal development. Some members of these resistance groups are also members of the security forces, both the National Police Force (*Polícia Nacional de Timor-Leste* – PNTL) and the Falintil-National Defence Force of Timor-Leste (*Falintil-Força de Defeza de Timor-Leste* – F-FDTL). It is important that these security institutions cooperate with each other to eliminate any competition between them, so that differences that may exist among the members of the police and the military, as well as among resistance groups and martial arts groups, do not exacerbate the security situation. Peace-building and conflict management require communication and engagement among different elements of society, which fought for independence, and now want to contribute to the security of Timor-Leste.

Since the intervention by the International Force for East Timor (INTERFET) in September 1999, which was led by the Australian Defence Forces against the brutal actions of the Indonesian military and the Indonesian-supported militias, the security sector of Timor-Leste has been under the responsibility of different international forces. After the restoration of independence on 20 May 2002, responsibility for the security sector was returned to the Timorese security institutions, i.e. the PNTL and the F-FDTL, two years later on 20 May 2004. Just two years later, the security situation collapsed as tensions between the PNTL and the F-FDTL led to a crisis in 2006. Since then, ordinary Timorese citizens have lost their confidence in the ability of the security institutions to protect society. There are two principle reasons for this loss of confidence: first, the security sector has been politicised by politicians who use security forces for their own agendas; and, second, there are many internal divisions among members of the security forces, depending on geographical affiliations, martial arts group membership, political connections, and mestizo-indigenous relations.

Historical Background

Timor-Leste has a tortured history. After 450 years of oppressive and neglectful Portuguese colonial rule, Timorese people fought each other in a brutal civil war in 1975.[1] Faced with increasing covert infiltration by neighbouring Indonesia, the East Timorese hastily declared independence on 28 November 1975. It was a short-lived 'state'. Two weeks after the national flag was raised, Indonesia invaded and annexed the territory in December 1975. During twenty-four years of brutal occupation, 183,000 people were killed or died of deprivation.[2] In 1999, the United Nations Mission in East Timor (UNAMET) supervised a 'Popular Consultation' in which 78.5 per cent of Timorese voted for independence. In the ensuing violence, Indonesian security forces and their Timorese militias killed 1,500 people, causing half of the population to flee their homes, and forcibly relocating 250,000 people to West Timor in Indonesia. The violence destroyed 70 per cent of the buildings in the country.[3]

Between 1999 and 2002 the United Nations Transitional Administration in East Timor (UNTAET) administered the territory with sovereign powers. This included responsibility for developing a new police force. UNTAET supervised the Constituent Assembly elections in August 2001, in which the Revolutionary Front for the National Liberation of East Timor (*Frente Revolucionária de Liberatação Nacional de Timor-Leste* – FRETILIN), led by its president, Fransisco 'Lu Olo' Guterres, and the Secretary-General Mari Alkatiri, won an absolute majority and subsequently formed the first government of the new state. The presidential elections were held in April 2002, and a resistance leader, Xanana Gusmão, became the first president. During the UNTAET period, powers were slowly devolved to Timorese officials, but ultimate sovereign power rested with the United Nations. This had critically important ramifications for the Timorese security sector, especially the police service and defence force.

On 20 May 2002 Timor-Leste's independence was restored, however, executive powers over internal security and external defence remained vested in UNTAET's successor mission, the United Nations Mission in Support of East Timor (UNMISET). It was only on 20 May 2004 that full sovereignty, as well as complete control over the security sector, was handed over to the Government of the Democratic Republic of Timor-Leste (G-RDTL).

The primary institutions in Timor-Leste's security sector are young, being less than a decade old. Although these institutions have achieved some successes, they have also suffered some serious setbacks and failures, and cannot yet be considered fully matured. In March 2000, the PNTL was formed, with the majority of its new recruits being young men and women. Contentiously, UNTAET recruited a number of the senior commanders from a cadre of senior officers drawn from the ranks of former Indonesian Police Force (POLRI).[4]

In February 2001, the former independence guerrilla force, Falintil, was transformed into the national defence force, F-FDTL. The manner in which UNTAET oversaw the establishment and recruitment of F-FDTL was a source of major discontent in Timorese society,[5] and became an influential catalyst in the creation and expansion of politically active veteran's groups across Timor-Leste. These groups were also highly critical of the PNTL, particularly because of the presence of a large number of former POLRI officers in the PNTL. Clashes between these groups and the PNTL caused serious security concerns in 2002 and 2003.

Neither the PNTL nor the F-FDTL was provided with substantive national executive civilian oversight by UNTAET. As a result, the policy-making, legislative and budgeting capacity of these organisations was virtually nil at the time of independence. While the Ministry of Interior grew rapidly between 2002 and 2004 under the controversial tutelage of the former Minister of Interior, Rogerio Lobato, the Office of the Secretary of State for Defence languished under the moribund leadership of Roque Rodrigues. Between 2004 and 2006 the PNTL became increasingly factionalised as a result of Rogerio Lobato's machinations, while F-FDTL's material and organisational conditions, poor to begin with, never improved.

Challenges for an Infant Country

Being a young, post-conflict country, Timor-Leste faces several challenges in the governance of its security sector. The first of these challenges is the resistance mentality that has proliferated throughout the country. For many people, the most prevalent thought in their minds was "Independence, or Death!" The Timorese are strong people, as proven by their success in the twenty-four years of struggle against a much more powerful Indonesia. However, the thinking required for revolution and the thinking required for developing a society are quite different, and thus, developing society requires a transformation in mentality. This is not an easy task, especially when the people have to rebuild their attitudes, while they must simultaneously rebuild the cities, towns, and villages that were burned down by the Indonesian military and its militias. Many of these militias are still organised and ready to mobilise, just across the border in West Timor, posing a material threat to the future security of Timor-Leste.

Another challenge revolves around the presence of a large number of resistance groups, which were formed during the years of armed resistance. Once the fighting was over, they lost their raison d'être, and needed to find something else to do: being well organised, these groups have continued to exist. Now, with a high unemployment rate, these groups are susceptible to manipulation and agitation by different political actors who seek their own personal gains. The most powerful political actors in Timor-Leste have control over many of these groups, being able to deploy them whenever necessary, regardless of whether their actions are legal or not. These groups, because of their connections with the political elite, can carry out these actions without worrying about legal repercussions. It is often said that in Timorese society, it is not the rule of law that dominates, but the rule of the deal.[6] As long as these groups exist, and are not being directed to positive activities or given enticing employment opportunities, they will be ready to act on behalf of those political actors who can pay and protect them. One might wonder whether or not economic development has been deliberately stunted as a way of keeping these groups around for future use.

Another challenge can be found in the recruitment of the members of the PNTL. The United Nations recruited many young people into the force who are members of the various martial arts groups in Timor-Leste. These police officers bring with them not only their group's mentality, but also maintain a deep sense of loyalty to that group. Imagine a situation in which the PNTL are called to a neighbourhood where fighting between two martial arts groups was reported. Two PNTL offices arrive at the scene and find that one of them belongs to one side, while the other officer belongs to the other side. One can easily see how difficult it may be to expect the PNTL to conduct professional police work in such a situation. Due to the presence of police officers affiliated with martial arts groups, the investigation process, such as the collection of evidence, interviewing of witnesses, and the processing of suspects, may be compromised.

The generation gap in Timor-Leste also contributes to the challenges of the security sector. Most of the older generation are closely affiliated with the Portuguese language, because they grew up in the colonial period, and were already adults when the independence struggle began. Also, many Falintil commanders were trained by the Portuguese army. Now, after having achieved independence, this generation of older Timorese uses the language situation as a way of holding on to power. Despite the fact that most Timorese do not speak Portuguese, it was made an official language for the country and the government. Many see this as a way of excluding the younger generations from participating in important political dialogues, and ensuring for the time being, that the older Portuguese-speaking politicians maintain their grip on the most important and influential political positions. A typical example of such a conspiracy can be found in the manipulation of the judicial system.

From the outset, the courts relied almost exclusively on international, usually UN-funded, Portuguese-speaking judicial actors. Excessive delays in investigations and prosecutions quickly undermined the credibility of the justice system, which functioned sporadically, if at all, in the three district courts outside Dili. These early failings further compounded public mistrust in the formal judicial process, which is still widely seen as exclusive by the majority of the population due to its legal complexity and the use of Portuguese (sometimes translated, mistranslated or paraphrased) in trial proceedings and prosecutorial investigations.[7]

Adding to the mistrust of the justice system is the prevailing impunity for those who have committed crimes in the past. Those few individuals who were brought before the court and received jail sentences were pardoned or released by the leaders of the government. These actions often violate the Constitution and are carried out without following proper judicial procedures. Disrespect for the law by the political elite increases the feeling that there is no justice for the common people, as long as political elites can intervene to ensure judicial outcomes in their favour.

In the absence of justice, people will turn to what they know and to what works. In Timor-Leste, that means using methods of conflict resolution from within their culture. "The lack of access to justice, compounded by the lack of adequate police response and investigative capacity, is a main contributing factor to the widespread reliance of communities on traditional or informal justice mechanisms."[8] Most Timorese speak at least three languages: Tetun, the lingua franca of Timor-Leste; the local language spoken in their home district; and, because of the Indonesian occupation, Indonesian. If the decision regarding the official languages were based purely on practical considerations, then Portuguese would not have been included in the list of official languages.

Another challenge the language situation poses, related to the security sector, is that of training for the police. Many police from Portugal are in Timor-Leste to train the PNTL. However, the language policy interferes with the efficiency of the training programmes. Before arriving in Timor-Leste, these Portuguese police officers were told that almost all the Timorese could speak Portuguese. Once they arrived in Timor-Leste, they realised that this was not the case, and the difficulties began. It was often the case that the language assistants (interpreters and translators) provided to these Portuguese police did not have sufficient language competency. This forces the PNTL to deal with at least three languages when conducting investigations, interrogations, and taking witness statements. Tetun is translated into English, which is then translated into Portuguese, and then the process is reversed. During the process of translation, some important details are doomed to be changed, adjusted or lost outright. In an institution that demands a focus on minute details and the collection of facts, such a problem of interpretation is counterproductive. Not only does it hamper police-work, but it also takes up crucial time that should be used for the training and instruction of PNTL officers. Without a serious reconsideration of the language policy in Timor-Leste, the problems stemming from using Portuguese as an official language will continue to pose a challenge for the development of the security sector.

Dimensions of the Country's Security Sector

Statutory Security Actors

The PNTL: The clandestine resistance was made up of many different groups such as martial arts groups, traditional arts groups, and youth groups. At the same time, some Timorese were also serving in the Indonesian military and police. All these groups were political by nature and well organised, and some were armed.

When the United Nations formed the PNTL it was from these groups that new police officers were recruited. The attempt to form a unified police force with a clear structure and chain of command was made difficult for several reasons. For example, the length of training was insufficient: new recruits were only given training for three months at the academy, which was not long enough to supplant loyalties to other organisations, their leadership and hierarchy.

It was also difficult to unify recruits from rival groups with competing interests, especially among those whose loyalties had been forged through a long period of conflict, struggle and insecurity. For many of these new police recruits, security was associated with belonging to their organisation, and they did not dare to provide security for the community as police officers. This gave the PNTL an unprofessional image in the eyes of the community. Many see the PNTL as discriminately protecting their own organisation rather than protecting the public in general.

Table 1: PNTL Personnel Breakdown[9]

Unit	Total	Male	Female	Unit	Total	Male	Female
Aileu	92	70	22	Viqueque	137	112	27
Ainaro	101	82	19	Immigration	83	70	13
Baucau	176	121	55	URP (Reserve)	81	80	1
Bobonaro	132	89	43	UPF (Border Patrol)	240	227	13
Covalima	130	100	30	Dili/UIR (Rapid Response)	143	137	6
Dili	452	361	91	Baucau/UIR (Rapid Response)	47	46	1
Ermera	131	101	30	International Police	3	3	0
Lautem	148	114	34	Police Academy	92	81	11
Liquica	101	76	25	Marine Unit	50	48	2
Manatuto	104	83	21	National HQ	499	416	83
Manufahi	109	92	17	**Total**	3,168	2,591	577
Oecusse	115	82	33				

Because of the lack of unity, the PNTL collapsed quite easily during the 2006 crisis. As protests grew more rowdy, the PNTL was unable or unwilling to control the situation. Some PNTL officers and petitioners were members of the protesting organisation and this led some to abandon their police duties and join the protesters. The origin of the crisis lay in perceived regional discrimination against those from the western region of Timor-Leste. As most of the PNTL officers were recruited from the western region, the same region the protesters were from, it was not surprising to see that the PNTL as an institution basically collapsed. As PNTL members joined those from the west who were protesting, the crisis took on an East versus West and F-FDTL versus PNTL character.

While both security sector institutions have become relatively stable since the crisis, the PNTL remains a fragile institution because the loyalties of its members are divided among a number of other organisations with alternative power structures and hierarchy outside the control of the government. As long as the loyalty of police officers is devoted to other groups, the PNTL will have a difficult time establishing itself as a unified organisation that can effectively provide security for all Timorese. Although the PNTL is tasked with assuming police responsibilities in the communities (community policing), it has become a militarised force under the new commander, Longuinhos Monteiro, appointed in March 2009. Table 1 (on page 156) shows the breakdown of PNTL personnel for 2009, while Table 2 (on page 158) shows the breakdown of the PNTL Community Police Unit by districts and types of activities for 2010. As declared by the government, the PNTL is responsible for dealing with internal threats in Timor-Leste.

The F-FDTL: The responsibility of F-FDTL is to secure the nation from any and all external threats. However, they have also been deployed on occasion in joint operations against security threats inside Timor-Leste. After the shooting of President José Ramos-Horta in February 2008, the F-FDTL and the PNTL cooperated in an operation to find Gastão Salsinha, and his group, who were in the mountains of Timor-Leste's interior. The F-FDTL was also deployed alongside the PNTL for several months in the western districts of Bobonaro and Covalima in response to reports of groups of armed ninjas harassing the public.

In peacetime, the F-FDTL helps the government by responding to any difficulties that arise during natural disasters. Recently they have begun implementing engineering projects on behalf of the government by building schools. This cooperation is strengthening the relationship between civilians and the military. This is the first step by the F-FDTL in actively contributing to development in peacetime.

Table 2: PNTL Community Police Unit[10]

District	Officers	Types of Activities
Aileu	3	Cooperate with UNPOL, visits to schools and villages, and meetings with communities to prevent criminal actions
Ainaro	3	Village visits, and meetings with the ex-petitioners and martial arts groups
Bobonaro	3	Village visits, and meetings with the ex-petitioners and martial arts groups
Baucau	3	Visits to schools and villages to prevent conflict and crime
Covalima	3	Cooperate with UNPOL, visits to schools and villages, and meetings with communities and local authorities to prevent criminal actions
Dili	9	Cooperate with UNPOL, visits to schools and villages to meet with communities and local authorities, also attending community meetings
Ermera	3	Along with university students visits to villages to meet with petitioners, and solving domestic violence issues
Lautem	3	Visit to villages and meetings with local leaders and attending the Christmas party
Liquica	3	Along with the local government promote civic education on Human Rights and HIV/AIDS
Manatuto	3	Along with UNPOL, visits to villages and meetings with the community about local government activities and monitoring projects that the government contracts to the private sector, like irrigation, road maintenance, and building construction
Oecussie	3	Along with UNPOL, visits to schools and villages, and meeting with community leaders
Viqueque	3	Visits to schools and villages to prevent conflict and crimes

Non-State Security Actors

As the armed wing of the national liberation struggle, the veterans of Falintil are often considered to be members of the security sector. Since independence veterans have frequently reminded the country of the power and influence they wield. Veterans played an active role in the 2006 crisis, with many of them being issued weapons and uniforms by the head of the military and the Minister of Defence. It is therefore important to focus on the role of the veterans in the Timorese security sector, especially with regard to their activities during and since the crisis.

The 2006 political crisis posed a serious threat to Timor-Leste, and also had a strong effect on the unity formed by veterans during their time of war. The unrest started with the allegation of ethnic discrimination within the Timor-Leste's Defence Force, and 159 members of the F-FDTL left their barracks protesting against favouritism for soldiers originating from the eastern part of the country. The number of soldiers leaving their posts increased to 594 – almost a half of the nation's defence force – significantly affecting national security at the height of the crisis. Some people blamed the protestors as the trigger of the crisis, while others blamed the incompetence of the organs of the state in dealing with the issue within the country's defence force. However, to date there has been no in-depth investigation into the 2006 crisis[11] and no public statement by political leaders in relation to the root causes of the problem.

Veterans, particularly those who joined Falintil and the clandestine movement, should have gone through a process of disarmament, demobilisation and reintegration (DDR). There is a need to acknowledge that the struggle of the veterans is valued, through a process of reparations and rehabilitation in all its aspects, including helping facilitate the return of veterans into civilian life. Despite the fact that the National Parliament has approved a veterans' law,[12] the demobilisation process was very slow, as there were many issues regarding the data verification process. However, the government has awarded some veterans medals. The government now has to face veterans' organisations such as *Sagrada Familia* (Holy Family), and Committee for the Popular Defence of the Democratic Republic of Timor-Leste (CPD-RDTL), as well as former combatants' organisations, such as Colimau 2000. A thorough investigation into the nature of these organisations needs to be conducted since they still have grass-root support in the community.

As a strong political power, veterans were involved in the 2006 crisis both directly and indirectly. Given the fact that they are not yet demobilised, it is worth considering involving them as reservists of the national security forces and thereby tasking them to protect the country from any threat.[13]

The definition of a veteran used in this chapter is as follows: a person who actively contributed to the war or struggled against Indonesian occupation to defend the country's independence.[14] It refers not only to former Falintil soldiers, but may also include civilians involved in the struggle on both the clandestine and diplomatic fronts. For those involved on the diplomatic front, the transition to normal life was not so problematic.[15] Hence, the veterans who need special attention are those who left the army to become civilians after the transformation of Falintil to F-FDTL. In order to identify them as veterans, an important factor is looking at the duration of their active involvement in the resistance, meaning the longest serving veterans will be those who were involved since 1975, both as civilian activists or Falintil soldiers. In a nutshell, the veterans are those who were active in the period sometime after the invasion of Indonesia until the independence of the country.

In addition to the veterans' group, there are other groups that need to be regarded as security sector actors in Timor-Leste, such as Force 2020. Although there is no clear-cut definition of Force 2020, it has a strong connection with the veterans and it was armed during the 2006 crisis, an action reminiscent of what happened on 20 August 1975.[16] However, some view this group as reservists (i.e. part of a statutory security force), rather than as a non-statuary security force. This may create confusion, because there is also a strategic vision for the F-FDTL,[17] which is commonly dubbed as Força 2020 (Force 2020).[18]

State Oversight Institutions

The President of Timor-Leste: José Ramos-Horta conducted a peacebuilding dialogue in the country during his presidency, travelling to all districts and visiting local people to discuss peacebuilding efforts in Timor-Leste. This dialogue programme was established in 2008 with the objective of reducing conflict between groups from different communities. These conflicts included those between *lorosae* (East) and *loromonu* (West), pro-autonomy and pro-independence, martial arts groups, veterans organisations, women and youth organisations, and the mestizos and indigenous. The president also made an effort to promote peace by naming the city of Dili, the "*Cidade Dili de Paz*", or the "City of Peace", and calling Atauro Island, "Ilha de Paz", or "Island of Peace." Another initiative by the president was the 2010 Ramelau Cultural Festival, which was held on the highest mountain in Timor-Leste called Ramelau: Ramos-Horta stated that he believes Ramelau can be a unifying symbol for all Timorese. In October 2011 the president worked with a Norwegian, Bishop Gunnar, in a series of meetings with members of different political parties in an effort to establish a national consensus on justice and reconciliation.[19]

National Parliament: While the National Parliament has approved the National Commission B to draft laws related to the security sector in Timor-Leste, they have yet to pass or implement any effective measures for reform. At the moment the possibility of drafting laws in the future is under discussion, but due to a lack of human resources, the pace of the process is slow.

Anti-Corruption Commission (Komisaun Anti-Korupsaun – KAK): The law that was approved on 29 June 2009 by the National Parliament created the KAK, which aims to create state competence for a specialised criminal police. The KAK's action will be based only on the criteria of legality and objectivity in articulation with the competent authorities, as it is important for its credibility as a mechanism to combat corruption. The KAK is fully independent from the executive body of the government of Xanana Gusmão and reports to the National Parliament. According to the criminal code, the KAK has the power to begin and conduct criminal investigations related to corruption. Moreover, it has an equally important role as a means of education and public sensitisation, by identifying and promoting the measures that prevent corruption.[20]

Non-State Oversight Institutions

Hukum Asasi Kemanusiaan (HAK): HAK is engaged in monitoring Timorese security forces' human rights violations against civilians. Not only do they research and publish reports on these violations, but they also provide human rights training to Timorese security institutions, in support of the professionalisation of the security forces.

Fundasaun Mahein: Fundasaun Mahein is the only NGO whose sole focus is the reform of the Timorese security sector. The activities of Fundasaun Mahein are concentrated on creating a space for public participation in the discussion of security sector issues. On the basis of interviews with a broad range of people from Timorese society, and through extensive research, it publishes in-depth reports on current security sector issues, and provides recommendations that are believed to have a positive effect in the security sector, and thereby Timorese society. Fundasaun Mahein operates based on a belief that the people have a right to engage in the development of their security institutions. There is, with the exception of some specific programmes, little or no structured or systematic civil society activity engagement with the Timorese security sector. Fundasaun Mahein seeks to fill this gap in the ranks of Timorese civil society by providing full-time monitoring and reporting on issues relating to the development of Timorese security sector in a manner which increases citizen participation in the process. Its mission is to strengthen and develop the security sector so that it can provide safety and thus prosperity to all Timorese citizens. In addition, it aims to increase the capacity of the media, other NGOs, and wider civil society to substantively engage in public policy issues relating to the security sector in a more informed, impartial and constructive manner.[21]

The Media: In Timor-Leste, the media have played a very significant role in helping the public access information regarding security sector issues. Through diligent investigation and research, they provide information, which might otherwise be withheld by the government. The weekly newspaper *Tempo Semanal* has a reputation for discovering and sharing information about government activities that enable the public to maintain a better understanding of current events in Timor-Leste. Investigative journalism is crucial to guaranteeing stability, democracy, and accountability, especially in post-conflict societies.

The Catholic Church: Another non-state institution that plays a significant role in providing oversight of the security sector in Timor-Leste is the Catholic Church. The Timorese are predominantly Catholic, and the Catholic Church's ability to engage with the youth – especially on issues of capacity building, conflict prevention, and non-violence – helps raise the awareness of the public about peacebuilding activities and how they affect society. *Cruz Joven* (literally,

"Youth Cross") is an organised youth activity, in which a cross is carried from church to church by young people from the surrounding area, and a discussion about peace, love, non-violence, community building, and capacity development is held. After these discussions, the participants return to their home villages and towns to enlighten their neighbours about what they have learned.

Challenges of the Security Sector in Timor-Leste

Transformation of Falintil to F-FDTL

During the struggle for independence, some leaders pondered an independent Timor-Leste without its own armed forces. "Timor-Leste shall be a peace-loving country. Timor-Leste shall ban the use of weapons in the territory and shall be a force to promote harmony amongst its citizens", wrote Xanana Gusmão.[22] This proposal echoed a similar proposal put forward by the former president, José Ramos-Horta. However, there was also another line of thought focusing on how to handle the role of the veterans after the war. There was also impetus to create an armed force to counter militias still threatening Timor-Leste from across the border, even though at that time it was believed that this problem could be handled through diplomatic measures with Indonesia. Another urgent reason was the necessity to create job opportunities for veterans of Falintil. Faced with these new realities, resistance leaders rapidly changed their views, and the establishment of armed forces seemed relevant.

Following in the footsteps of other post-colonial countries, the nation-building process in Timor-Leste was subject to strong political intervention from former colonial countries, through UNTAET. Almost the entire development of the country's defence force was spearheaded by UNTAET, whose lack of understanding of the local context and realities directly contributed to the 2006 crisis. As an institution with overarching powers, UNTAET held both legislative and executive authority in Timor-Leste.

INTERFET was not mandated to collect weapons belonging to the militias and no agreement was made in relation to the existence of the Falintil. The head of UNTAET gave permission for members of Falintil to carry their weapon within the cantonment area in Aileu but not beyond it.[23] In the cantonment area, the number of Falintil eventually rose to 5,000. UNTAET itself was not tasked to set up the country's armed forces. However, after a conference of the National Council for Timorese Resistance (*Conselho Nacional de Resistência Timorense* – CNRT) in March 2000, INTERFET, UNTAET and Falintil discussed the reintegration of former Falintil members into civilian life. Cooperation involving both INTERFET/UNTAET and Falintil was intended to support the formation of a professional armed force for Timor-Leste after the mission of INTERFET/UNTAET expired.[24] Driven by this goal, UNTAET commissioned King's College London to carry out a study, which was submitted to UNTAET on 8 August 2000. The study presented three options for the future development of the country's armed forces.[25]

The first option, which was Falintil's preference, was to form an armed force ranging from 3-5,000 soldiers. The second option called for a regular force of 3,000 soldiers with almost one half of the force composed of former guerrilla fighters. The third option was similar to the second option, there were to be 3,000 soldiers recruited, but half of them would be former members of Falintil. From these three options, King's College recommended the third option, taking into account the security situation in the country, as well as the need to boost economic growth in the country.[26] This left almost two thirds of the former guerrillas out of the regular forces, although whenever necessary, they could be called on as reservists to fight alongside the regular forces against any security threats.

According to UNTAET Regulation No. 1/2001 (UNTAET/REG/2001/1), after consulting with the National Council – a mini-parliament then chaired by Xanana Gusmão – UNTAET and the East Timor Transitional Administration (ETTA) began to discuss the future establishment of F-FDTL in September 2000, on the basis of the study from King's College.[27] During a donor's conference on 20-21 November 2000, Australia and Portugal expressed their willingness to support the development of the F-FDTL.[28] The recruitment of the first battalion of the F-FDTL was carried out on 29 June 2001, with the bulk of its members being recruited from former guerrilla fighters, most of who were from the eastern part of the country. Later, when the second battalion was formed in 2002, individuals over 21 were recruited, and many of them had not taken part in the struggle for independence.

If we thoroughly analyse the process of transformation from Falintil to F-FDTL, we can see there were many problems that remained unsolved, including the ones identified by those opposed to, and critical of, the process. Some even said that the recruitment was not transparent in the eyes of the public because the process was not carried out under a democratic system. In addition, the proposal aimed for the establishment of a professional armed force, but according to this criterion alone, many former guerrillas were excluded due to their past experience as guerrillas. They thus had to be reintegrated into society through the reintegration programme run by the International Organisation of Migration (IOM), with financial support from the World Bank. This meant former guerrillas, after undergoing various brief vocational training courses, were sent home with a tiny amount of money to start up their own small businesses. Given the fact that most of the veterans were trained on how to use weapons, rather than to manage a business, it proved hard for them to start new lives. A United Nations Children's Funds (UNICEF) report describes how the youth that had joined Falintil and the clandestine front later felt that they were sidelined from the development process of the country for which they had given so much of their lives: most had spent almost all of their time in the jungle, unable to continue their studies because they never had time to learn.[29]

A part of the problem was that the recruitment process interrupted the strong relationship between the people and Falintil, which was still seen as a liberation force.[30] Major General Taur Matan Ruak said that the F-FDTL was not a perfect place for young people looking for jobs, and anyone wanting to join it had to think twice. Taur Matan Ruak was somewhat sceptical about the commitment of the future government to the defence force. He added that as a liberation force, the F-FDTL was ready to transform itself into a modern institution in a relatively short period, as a response to the demands of the international community, willing to assist in the creation of a defence institution based on western standards.[31]

Thus, the recruitment process itself did not benefit the veterans who had spent most of their lives with Falintil, because most of them failed to meet the physical and health criteria to join the new military. There were also problems related to the ranking structure because some of those who were commanders in the jungle were demoted, while those who worked as informants or mail-men were promoted to officers' ranks, such as captain, due to their educational background, and without having contributed much to Falintil's struggle for independence. This made some former fighters prefer to return to civilian life. Those commanders who left the F-FDTL included, from the western part of the country, Commander Samba 9 and Commander Ernesto Dudu, and from the eastern part, Secretary Renan Selac and Commander Eli Foho Rai Boot, aka L-7.[32]

Another doubt about the plans formulated in the King's College study was the lack of consideration for the specifics of the history, which threatens to ruin the F-FDTL in the long run. For instance, the King's College report proposal on reservists, stating that they are to serve "voluntarily", caused various misleading interpretations, and contributed to the formation of the problematic Force 2020, which deployed during the 2006 crisis. A leader of the F-FDTL, Brigadier General Lere Anan Timur, said that those who were involved in the force were those who were armed and most of them were former guerrillas and clandestine front members who had struggled for the country's independence, and whose spirit of nationalism and patriotism should not be questioned.[33]

Considering all this, the King's College study had numerous limitations. In particular, when advising the formation of an armed force, it did not take into account the perspectives of those who had been involved directly in the struggle, but instead confined its consultations to certain political leaders. These problems explain why there were protests from former guerrilla members and clandestine movement groups, such as Sagrada Familia, Colimau 2000 and CPD-RDTL, that the transformation of the Falintil to F-FDTL failed to capture the historical value of the Falintil.[34]

Problematic Veterans: Reintegration into Civilian Life

In September 2008, veterans numbered 75,143 according to the government, and of that figure, some 13,889 have been granted recognition for their fight, while some 12,538 have received veteran's funds from the government.[35]

The veterans are now widespread across the social economic landscape. Apart from the F-FDTL, they are in the government occupying important positions, and officers within the PNTL. They are also involved in various political parties, active as members of parliament, and some have become businessmen. Some of them joined organisations such as Sagrada Familia, Colimau 2000, CPD-RDTL and other resistance organisations.

This pattern shows that those who were part of the armed struggle now have to compete with other citizens to have a normal life, as part of their reintegration into society; although some are also inclined to use their political power to advance their interests. To some extent, veterans are seen as patrons of the process of liberation and therefore the status has a certain reverence to it, with the respectful title of 'big brother' being applied to veterans. Because of this relationship, in which they see themselves as superior to the rest of the society, Xanana Gusmão is more often called 'brother number one' instead of prime minister, which situates him and other veterans more as past warriors, instead of public servants of the state.[36]

Analysis of Leadership Influence

SSG in Timor-Leste remains a major challenge, as the process has been politicised by multiple political factions. Three major factors include: Xanana Gusmão's network, FRETILIN and the general influence veterans have on security sector development in Timor-Leste.

Xanana Gusmão's Network: The first factor is the current prime minister, Xanana Gusmão, who is the dynamic and charismatic former commander of the guerrilla army, Falintil. Gusmão is revered for his political savvy and his leadership during the resistance. While these traits served him well against the Indonesians, his leadership style has often clashed with those wishing to see a more open and democratic society in post-independence Timor-Leste. Gusmão oftentimes ignores legal frameworks and the Constitution when making decisions. A recent major issue was the release of former militia leader, Maternus Bere. After being captured by the people of Suai – the town where his militia massacred over 200 people at a church – he was handed over to the government in Dili. Under the guise of maintaining good relations with Indonesia, Gusmão had him released.

The decision to release Bere, almost ten years after independence, received widespread criticism from the Timorese people and international partners as well. Many felt it was a serious blow to the development of a security and justice sector, already hampered by allegations of impunity. One survivor of the Suai massacred summed up this point in simple eloquence: "So if one day I get another member of the Laksaur Militia, I will make my own judgment, with my own hand."[37]

Another example of ignoring the Constitution includes Gusmão's relationship with the PNTL. Despite regulations being put in place, and the passing of a PNTL Organic Law, some police officers without the proper education or training are being promoted to high-ranking positions, over more qualified candidates. This, along with a political appointee to the position of Commander General of PNTL, shows that Gusmão has consistently forced his decisions upon the people, regardless of their legality.

Having become the prime minister by organising a coalition called the Parliamentary Majority Alliance (AMP), Gusmão had to distribute many posts to politicians from different parties to reward them for their help in forming the coalition, which made the government sluggish and less willing to fight corruption. Another consequence is the use of political appointees to fill specialised positions.

In 2009, former Prosecutor General Longuinhos Monteiro was appointed by Gusmão to be Commander General of PNTL. Many saw this as rewarding a loyal friend, and as Gusmão's way of balancing the power between the F-FDTL and the PNTL. This appointment, however, violated the 2008 PNTL Organic Law, which requires the Commander General to be a police officer, which Monteiro is not. Another criticism against Gusmão's decision pointed to the tendency of PNTL to become more militarised since Monteiro took power. During his inauguration ceremony, Monteiro rode in on a large bright-blue armoured personnel carrier in a military style parade featuring police officers with automatic weapons. It is pertinent here to note briefly that when studying at a university in Indonesia, Monteiro participated in the Indonesian military's university student training programme, and that this is the suspected source of his fondness for military flair. This has alarmed the Timorese people, and caused the relationship between the PNTL and the F-FDTL to remain tense.[38]

FRETILIN: FRETILIN is the largest, and most popular political party, especially in rural districts and at the grassroots level, and is capable of organising a large crowd of people for political gatherings. Political manoeuvring and the violence of the 2006 crisis forced FRETILIN out of power. Indeed, Alfredo Reinado, who was one of the main actors in the crisis, said, "I don't care if I die tomorrow [...] But before I go I want to see Alkatiri put on trial for the crimes he has committed [...] Xanana is my commander-in-chief and I will obey his orders as long as he remains on the (side of) right".[39] Currently FRETILIN is the opposition party due to the efforts of Xanana Gusmão to organise a coalition of parties to take power. Much of the corruption within the government today is the product of this coalition, and the compromises made to ensure FRETILIN remained out of power. One of the lasting effects of the crisis is the further polarisation of the political elite, and the increasing importance politicians place on relationships with the security sector. Having been removed from power in the wake of the 2006 crisis and kept out after the 2007 and 2012 elections, FRETILIN leader Mari Alkatiri knows his party is still strong, and is establishing links across the political spectrum. Most importantly, FRETILIN is maintaining strong connections with members of PNTL and F-FDTL.[40]

Interference of political elites has a significant impact on SSG in Timor-Leste. While the PNTL and the F-FDTL continue to develop and professionalise their forces, they have to face up to attempts by the members of the political parties to politicise them. It was these two institutions (PNTL and F-FDTL) that were at the forefront of the 2006 crisis. FRETILIN knows the crisis was used by the opposition to gain power, and does not want this to happen again. Yet, mistakes already made, and the lack of progress in SSR, serve as a key agenda for FRETILIN when it criticises the current administration.

Veterans: Veterans of the resistance wield tremendous and extensive power across a broad spectrum of Timorese society. They are revered for their struggles in the bush, and their ability to maintain a guerrilla war against a vastly superior army whose numbers were high and whose weapons were better. After the 1999 referendum they felt they were mistreated and not respected by the international community, who governed the country under UNTAET. Many veterans were not employed in the security sector, and the formation of the military was highly politicised. This led to tensions between former resistance commanders who were left out and those who were given valuable posts in the government and the new military (F-FDTL). This became more evident in the 2006 crisis.

After the dispersal of protestors and the breakdown of order in Dili, it was the veterans to whom the government turned to restore order and provide security in Dili. With armed groups attacking the headquarters of the F-FDTL, as well as the residence of its head general, the military was called in and reinforced by Force 2020, the quasi-reserve force made up primarily of veterans and their families, who were given weapons and uniforms to assist the military in restoring order in 2006. This shows the power of the veterans over political outcomes.

Many of the veterans involved in the crisis are now influential members of the government. Cornelio Gama, aka L-7, and former Major Tara are both members of parliament now. L-7, along with veterans formerly under his command, was heavily involved in Force 2020 and is now the head of the Veterans' Political Party. Major Tara, who was a part of the protestors, is a member of the Social Democratic Party (PSD). Even Rai Los, who led the group that attacked the F-FDTL headquarters, has been rewarded with frequent business contracts in his home district of Liquica.

Another influential veteran is Fernando 'Lasama' Araujo. As the founder of the National Resistance of the Students of Timor-Leste (RENETIL), Lasama was heavily involved in organising the resistance within Indonesia, and spent time in Cipinang Prison for his activities, where he met Xanana Gusmão, who was a political prisoner. Lasama, who is the head of the Democratic Party (PD) and at the forefront of the next generation of political leaders in Timor-Leste, acted as the president of parliament from 2007-2012 and is currently the vice prime minister. He maintains a close relationship with PNTL General Commander Longuinhos Monteiro.[41]

Conclusion

This chapter reviewed the features and developments of SSG in Timor-Leste after the restoration of its independence in May 2002. It highlighted the challenges of its security sector, which were inherent to the early stages of peacebuilding, such as the transformation of Falintil (a non-state guerrilla force) to F-FDTL (a state military force); the reintegration of veterans into civilian life; and the political leadership's influence over the security sector in Timor-Leste. A close analysis of the challenges of SSG in Timor-Leste leads to the conclusion that proper treatment of non-state security actors, who have contributed to the struggle for independence and resistance, is as important as the proper management of state security actors.

Notes

1 The Commission for Reception, Truth and Reconciliation in Timor-Leste (CAVR), *Chega! The Report of the Commission for Reception, Truth and Reconciliation in Timor-Leste (CAVR), Executive Summary* (Dili: CAVR, 2005), p. 55.

2 *Ibid.*, p. 73.

3 *Timor-Leste Overview,* The World Bank, http://www.worldbank.org/en/country/timor-leste/overview.

4 Ludovic Hood, "Security Sector Reform in East Timor 1999-2004", *International Peacekeeping,* vol. 13, no. 1, March 2006, p. 64.

5 Edward Rees, *Under Pressure Falintil-Forcas de Defesa de Timor-Leste: Three Decades of Defence Force Development in Timor-Leste 1975-2004* (Geneva, April 2004), p. 3.

6 Informal discussion with Joanico Da Silva, Xefe Aldeia (Chief of Sub-Village), Surik Mas, December 2009.

7 The Centre for International Governance Innovation (CIGI), *Security Sector Reform Monitor: Timor-Leste,* No. 3, January 2011, p. 2.

8 *Ibid,* p. 14.

9 The Centre for International Governance Innovation (CIGI), *Security Sector Reform Monitor: Timor-Leste,* No. 1, December 2009, p. 7, http://www.cigionline.org/sites/default/files/SSRM%20-%20East%20Timor%20 -%201.pdf.

10 Information provided by PNTL Community Police Unit, Dili, 8 November 2010.

11 This fact was raised in the United Nations Independent Special Commission of Inquiry for Timor-Leste, which was strongly criticised by the FRETILIN party because the commission failed to refer to measures taken by the government. See the *Report of the United Nations Independent Special Commission of Inquiry for Timor-Leste* (Geneva: UNOCHA, October 2, 2006), and see also FRETILIN's Department of Information and Mobilization (DEPIM), *Nakroma Depim* (Dili: FRETILIN, 2006).

12 See, RDTL Constitution, Article 11, which provides a broad definition but does not specifically mention the process of disarmament, demobilisation and reintegration (DDR).

13 Interview with Lieutenant Colonel Sabika, 22 November 2010, and L-4, 27 November 2010.

14 Centro Estudo ba Dame no Dezenvolvimento (CEPAD), *Timor-Leste: Povu Nia Lian no Dalan ba Dame* (Dili: CEPAD/Interpeace, 2010). Veterans may also be defined as former workers of an institution or a company, who for reasons such as illness or injury, have been forced to leave the workplace. See Aderito José Guterres Correia, *Disionáriu Nasionál ba Tetum Ofisiál* (Dili: INL, 2005).

15 In the wake of further problems in relations with the veterans, Xanana Gusmão, asked former Falintil to reorganise themselves, highlighting that it was not important to distinguish clandestine and diplomatic fronts. See *Timor-Post,* 19 July 2010.

16 Interview with António Ai-Tahan Matak, 17 November 2010.

17 Força 2020 is based on the national vision of 2020. Its purpose is to establish a professional, modern armed force, which can guarantee the territorial security of Timor-Leste as its primary security mission. See Júlio Tomas Pinto, "Plano Força 2020: O mar e o futuro Timor-Leste", *Tempo Semanál,* vol. 4, no. 24, 15 June 2010.

18 Interview with L-4, 27 November 2010.

19 Further information about the President of Timor-Leste is available at: http://presidenttimorleste.tl/.

20 "Anti-Corruption Comission – ACC", Government of Timor-Leste, 12 March 2010, http://timor-leste.gov.tl/?p=60&n=1&lang=en.

21 For more information about Fundasaun Mahein, see "Fundasaun Mahein (FM)", The Association for Security Sector Education and Training (ASSET), http://ipcs.org/assetdemo/member_details.php?recNo=41.

22 Xanana Gusmão, wrote to the conference entitled "Indonesia setelah Suharto" organised by the Asia Foundation, and held at the University of Auckland, New Zealand, on 10 September 1998; his communication was read by Virgilio Guterres da Silva. Xanana Gusmão, "Timor-Leste Merdeka, Indonesia Bebas", in Tri Agus S. Siswowihardjo (ed.), *Solidamor* (Jakarta, 1999), p. 105, and p. 161.

23 "An Overview of FALINTIL's Transformation to FDTL and its Implications", *La'o Hamutuk Bulletin*, vol. 6, no. 1-2, April 2005, pp. 1-5, http://www.laohamutuk.org/Bulletin/2005/Apr/bulletinv6n1.html.

24 *Ibid.*

25 Centre for Defence Studies, King's College London, "Independent Study on Security Force Options and Security Sector Reform for East Timor," 8 August, 2000.

26 *Ibid.*

27 UNTAET, *Force Development Plan For The East Timor Defence Force 2001-2002* (Dili: UNTAET, 2002).

28 The UNTAET Regulation was legalised on 29 January 2001. See *La'o Hamutuk Bulletin,* Vol. 6, no. 1-2, April 2005, http://www.laohamutuk.org/Bulletin/2005/Apr/bulletinv6n1.html.

29 The citation in relation to the UNICEF's report is taken from Hilmar Farid, *Membangun Perdamaian di Timor-Lorosa'e,* a paper presented on the Conference on Peace and Disarmament, Universidade Dili (Dili University), 8-10 December 2002.

30 For further information on the relationship of "the fish and the water" between Falintil and the Timorese in general, see Siaran Pers, "'Ikan yang Semakin Jauh dari Air': Relasi Sipil dan Militer di Timor-Leste Pasca Kemerdekaana," *Mahein Nia Lian,* no 7, 6 July 2010, http://www.fundasaunmahein.wordpress.com.

31 *Ibid.*

32 Rahung Nasution, "Failed State and the Rise of Timor-Leste Burgeois", May 20, 2006, http://mauberedigitalarmy.wordpress.com/.

33 Interview with Lere Anan Timur, see *Kla'ak Semanál,* no. 32, 3 October 2008.

[34] The transformation from the Falintil to the F-FDTL triggered protests from former members of Falintil who had used the name for their group for such a long time: for instance, a group named Hanai Pai (Adore the Father) led by Labarik Maia. In some districts there were also isolated instances of members of Falintil disrupting the security of local people. See *Talitikum,* Edition 43, 29 July 2002.

[35] CEPAD, p. 68.

[36] See campaign fliers of the CNRT (*Conggreso Nacional de Reconstrução de Timor-Leste*) in 2008, which lauded Xanana Gusmão as a leader of the veterans instead of focusing more on his competence as prime minister of the government. This issue is not a matter of national discourse or featured in the national media.

[37] "Internet Exclusive: Maternus Bere Case - Breaking News: Bere has a VISA", *Tempo Semanal,* 24 September 2009, http://temposemanaltimor.blogspot.com/2009/09/internet-exclusive-maternus-bere-case.html.

[38] See Matt Crook, "East Timor: Political Appointment of Police Chief Resented", *Inter Press Service News Agency,* 22 March 2009, http://www.ipsnews.net/2009/03/east-timor-political-appointment-of-police-chief-resented/.

[39] Lindsay Murdoch, "How to end crisis: Timor rebel chief speaks out", *The Age,* 1 June 2006, http://www.theage.com.au/news/national/how-to-end-crisis-timor-rebel-chief-speaks-out/2006/05/31/1148956416797.html

[40] *Ibid.*

[41] International Crisis Group (ICG), "Timor Leste's Veterans: An Unfinished Struggle?" Asia Briefing No. 129 (Brussels: International Crisis Group, 2011), www.crisisgroup.org/~/media/Files/asia/south-east-asia/timor-leste/B129%20 Timor-Lestes%20Veterans%20-%20Unfinished %20Struggle.pdf.

Conclusion

YUJI UESUGI

This volume is a consolidated effort by experts from Asia to provide an overview of security sector governance (SSG) in the region. This initiative was inspired by the observation that Asia has been under-examined in the existing literature on security sector reform (SSR), which has also singularly failed to incorporate the views of experts from the region. It is hoped that this initiative will serve as a step to consolidate the further study of SSG and SSR in Asia.

In this respect, this concluding chapter should serve as a bridge to further research, which can widen and deepen our understanding of SSG as a component of peacebuilding in Asia. Hence, instead of providing a summary of findings from the case studies presented in this volume, the following seeks to pose a set of questions designed to provoke further inquiry into how divergent approaches, emanating from different disciplines and literatures, may be related to the theory and practice of SSR and peacebuilding in Asia.

Two Further Inquiries

There are contextual differences affecting each effort at SSR that lead to distinct challenges for SSG in each country examined. A close analysis of the six cases of this volume reveals, however, several recurring puzzles and paradoxes, illuminated as a result of multidisciplinary dialogue on the theme of SSG and peacebuilding in Asia. A set of thought-provoking inquiries can be reframed under the following two questions:

- How to overcome the dilemma of local/national ownership?
- Is democratisation a precondition for successful SSR?

How to Overcome the Dilemma of Local/National Ownership?

The case studies of this volume have illuminated the fact that the concept of local/national ownership in the context of SSR should be understood in terms of two dimensions: (1) the political will of the leadership (power-holding elite) of the country concerned to lead a genuine reform process; and (2) the capacity of the host government apparatus (and society) to undertake the reform process effectively. Hence, external support for SSR should aim to provide support (or pressure) not only to the host country's security sector institutions but also to the host government leadership as well. It does not pose a critical problem when the host country does not have sufficient capacity to carry out SSR, but its leaders have a genuine political will to undertake the necessary reform, because in such a case the international community can fill the capacity gap in the host country. In other words, the international community can serve as a substitute for local/national capacity. The most serious challenge is the lack of political will on the side of the host government. Indeed, at the heart of many unsuccessful attempts at SSR lies the attitude and mind-set of some opportunistic or devious elements within the political elite. Nevertheless, this important aspect of SSG has not been adequately addressed in current efforts at SSR, where the concept of local/national ownership has been used as an excuse for not interfering in the domestic affairs of the power centre of a host government.

The issues revolving around the political will of the leadership allude to the dilemma that exists between the pursuit for democratic governance (in which enhancing the accountability and integrity of the security sector is of the utmost priority) and respect for local/national ownership in SSR. There is a consensus among scholars and practitioners of SSR that local/national ownership is important for any SSR attempt to be sustainable. For example, the Geneva Centre for the Democratic Control of Armed Force (DCAF) argues that the role of external players in SSR is to *assist* the host government and society to maintain a legitimate and functioning security sector.[1]

However, the concept of local/national ownership is not synonymous with the concept of *laissez-faire*. Just simply and blindly yielding control of SSR to a local/national authority that is not capable or willing to undertake the necessary reform is not the right answer. If SSR is left in the hands of local/national leaders who seek to monopolise and manipulate the reform process in favour of their personal political ambitions (for example, by strengthening their power basis through SSR), the consequences would constitute a further threat to ordinary people, whose security and safety must be paramount in any genuine SSR agenda. This raises a series of questions: Who is the owner of the reform process? Is the host government (or political elite) representative of the true voices of the people? Whose views should be prioritised over others when several interests are diametrically opposed?

In the situation where the interests of ordinary people can easily be side-lined in order to promote the aspirations of a powerful elite, the international community should protect the interest of the most vulnerable and neglected groups in a society. It is in this area where the added value, as well as responsibility, of the international community lies in SSR support. Nonetheless, when external players try to impose a certain set of norms and rules upon the local government/society, SSR faces the challenge of confronting a lack of genuine local/national ownership, as well as the lack of political will to accept externally driven reform. As concerns SSR in the context of post-conflict state-building, the end of an armed conflict can signify a golden opportunity for proceeding with an 'externally defined, ideal reform', as a host country is more likely to be dependent on external support, and thus, more receptive to external involvement. As was seen in the case of Timor-Leste, the United Nations assumed much wider and more profound responsibilities in security sector development during the pre-independence period. In the post-independence period, however, the United Nations lost the initiative and its grip on the reform process once the local/national elite became confident of their power base within the government and beyond.

The case studies of countries in political transition, such as Indonesia, the Philippines and Thailand, showed that the reform process enjoyed a strong sense of local/national ownership and very limited roles for external players, such as the United Nations, existed. Moreover, Timor-Leste, Sri Lanka and to some extent Nepal, asserted a stronger sense of state sovereignty and did not hesitate to show their reluctance, if not resistance, to external intrusion.

Under such circumstances, there are two ways for the international community to safeguard the integrity of SSG in these countries. First and foremost, the international community can assist in a comprehensive reform agenda in such a way as to incorporate the four key agendas highlighted in this study: efforts to facilitate political reconciliation, to enhance the legitimacy of the government, to redefine proper civil-military relations, and to establish effective and accountable civilian oversight mechanisms. Second, the international community can assist in democratisation, which can entail a wider set of reforms beyond the security sector. Because SSR is highly political in nature and a part of a wider reform, it should be included in, and pursued as, an integral part of any agenda for democratisation. The sustained popular pressure that has emerged as a result of progress in democratisation in each country can bring internal pressure to bear on governments to undertake the necessary reform of the security sector and beyond.

Is Democratisation a Precondition for Successful SSR?

Autocratic rule coupled with patrimonial security actors often undermines and suppresses the genuine aspirations of the people for greater freedom and democracy. Hence, it is often understood that more effective SSG can contribute to and consolidate democratisation. In short, SSR is intuitively considered to be a precondition for democratisation. Hence, SSR has been included in a list of early peacebuilding tasks for United Nations peace operations in post-conflict countries, such as Nepal and Timor-Leste, so that SSR can pave the way for a much longer process of democratisation.[2] The linear and sequential application of several reform measures has dominated the strategic thinking around post-conflict peacebuilding. That is, SSR is regarded as a short-term task, and peacebuilding as a mid-term activity, with democratisation posed as a long-term endeavour to reach the goal of building a better society that upholds human security.

It is probably rational to conclude that successful SSR can contribute to conditions conducive to peacebuilding and democratisation. Perhaps, it can even consolidate a foundation for more sustainable peacebuilding and democratisation. However, this ought to be seen as a controversial proposition, judging from the case studies of this volume, which have indicated a possibility that democratisation is a primary process and it can serve as a mechanism for SSR to be institutionalised. Under conditions of democracy, implementing genuine SSR is easier, and the outcome of such an attempt is more likely to be up to the level of so-called 'international standards' than

SSR that is carried out under autocratic rule or immature democracy. For instance, against the backdrop of a nationwide democratisation process in Indonesia, a peace agreement was reached between the Government of Indonesia and the Free Aceh Movement (GAM) to terminate the localised conflict in Aceh, which allowed for SSR not only in Aceh but also in the broader national context. It shows that democratisation can pave the way for SSR, rather than the other way around. This is one example of counter-intuitive evidence found in the case of Indonesia.

If SSR is to be pursued as part of a wider democratisation process, then it has to be regarded as a long-term measure. If SSR is envisaged as an early imperative within a peacebuilding strategy, then it must also be considered a short-term measure. The findings of this study imply that it might be misleading to consider SSR to be a short-term measure that can act as a precondition for democratisation. This does not mean, however, that any attempts at SSR should be postponed in a situation where no sign of socio-political transformation exists. It is still debatable whether democratisation is an accelerating factor or a structural precondition for SSR. Nevertheless, what is clear, and what has also been demonstrated in this study, is that without being properly situated within a wider socio-political transformation, SSR is unlikely to guarantee the effectiveness and integrity of the security sector. The stagnation of the Nepalese SSR process is a case in point. The deadlock in democratisation (and in particular constitution-making) and the standstill in social transformation have prevented any meaningful progress in SSR. In other words, SSR should be pursued not only as a strategy of peacebuilding, but also as a part of a wider democratisation agenda.

Two Key Lessons

In addition, key lessons learned from the six cases examined in this volume can be highlighted here in the following two points: First, a failure of existing practices to incorporate a proper mechanism for dealing with non-state security actors in the peace agreement can entail a serious risk of undermining not only the implementation of the peace agreement, but also the post-agreement SSR process. The case of Timor-Leste is highly illustrative of the relative importance of non-state security actors in post-conflict peacebuilding. In fact, non-state security actors in Timor-Leste were able to destabilise the delicate political situation with nothing more than stones and knives in their hands. The same critique can be addressed to most existing literature on SSR, as it has focused predominantly on statutory security actors, such as the police and the military. Insufficient attention has been paid to non-state actors in the security sector, even though they play an important role in SSG, as the six cases examined in this volume demonstrate. Breakaway factions, such as those from former GAM combatants in Indonesia (Aceh), the Moro National Liberation Front (MNLF) and the Moro Islamic Liberation Front (MILF) in the Philippines, demobilised Maoist soldiers in Nepal, and former militias and Armed Forces for the National Liberation of East Timor (Falintil) combatants in Timor-Leste, should be brought to the centre of discussion on SSG in each country.

The issues of non-state security actors or ex-combatants have been dealt with within a framework of disarmament, demobilisation and reintegration (DDR), in which the emphasis has been placed on the issue of reintegration of ex-combatants, and thus the strategy of SSR vis-à-vis non-state security actors has been framed mainly in terms of economic language, such as providing jobs and livelihoods to ex-combatants. Nevertheless, this study suggests that non-state security actors should be included as targets of reform, because the de-politicisation of non-state security actors is equally as important as the de-politicisation and professionalisation of statutory security actors.

The second lesson is about the relevance and efficacy of the SSR approach in addressing certain obstacles in a peacebuilding process. For example, SSR may not be an appropriate tool for transforming socio-cultural structures, such as royalism and caste, which are serious obstacles against peacebuilding and democratisation in Thailand and Nepal, respectively. Under the circumstances, in which the root causes of stalled reform are embedded in socio-cultural systems of these countries, technical reform of the security sector will not be sufficient to foster their profound transformation. Another example of this dynamic can be found in the case of Sri Lanka, where issues of trust-building play a pivotal role in its peacebuilding endeavour. While appropriate SSR can contribute to solidifying the legitimacy of the government, and thus nurturing trust between the government and the minority communities, SSR might not be the most effective tool to reduce the discrimination that exists between majority and minority groups in the society. Furthermore, all the cases examined in this volume underline the importance of addressing the issue of political will of the host country's leadership, which has been placed outside the scope of regular SSR activities on the grounds that this may prejudice local/national ownership. Nevertheless, within nascent democracies, SSR might have to tackle the problems of autocratic rule by the democratically elected (but corrupted or immature) political elite, until those days when sensible citizens can remove them through democratic processes. This requires going beyond existing SSR parameters, and engaging more directly with the closely intertwined strategies and processes of democratisation.

Final Remarks

In sum, by examining the nexus between SSG and peacebuilding in Indonesia, the Philippines, Thailand, Nepal, Sri Lanka and Timor-Leste, this study underlines the importance of paying sufficient attention to democratic governance and the political dimensions of SSG. The study also shed light on the neglected, but perhaps the most important, actors in SSR, i.e. the political elite of a host country, as their behaviour and attitudes would affect the direction of political reconciliation, the quality of legitimacy of the government, the nature of civil-military relations, and the integrity of civilian oversight mechanisms. This study also indicated that in order for SSR to succeed in countries undergoing both political transition and post-conflict state-building, accelerating democratisation processes can be a key solution, as these countries are more likely to have weak civilian oversight mechanisms vis-à-vis their security forces. Therefore, the major challenge of SSG in the context of peacebuilding is to find a way to establish effective and accountable civilian oversight mechanisms, despite the fact that the focus of SSR has often been on primary security sector actors, such as the military and the police. Hence, SSR should be envisaged as an integral part of wider democratisation processes, whereby development of democratic institutions can facilitate SSR and vice versa.

In addition to the main focus of this study, this volume highlighted the important linkage between peacebuilding and democratisation, which has led to a debate about whether democratisation can be a means of peacebuilding in Asia. Experts remain divided as to whether democratisation should be considered a primary process. The point to be recapitulated and emphasised here is that an intuitive sequential development approach incorporating SSR, peacebuilding and democratisation needs to be questioned. Although this debate is not the main focus of this joint effort, and thus the relationship between democratisation and peacebuilding has not been explored thoroughly in this volume, this inquiry can improve our understanding of SSG in Asia. Furthermore, the thought-provoking inquiries presented here can facilitate more active academic discussion on the theme of SSG and peacebuilding in Asia, and as a result, SSR will be placed more firmly on academic agendas. It is expected that this study should serve as a first step towards such a goal and as an opportunity for dialogue between academics and practitioners of SSR.

Notes

1 *SSR in a Nutshell. Manual for Introductory Training on Security Sector Reform*, (Geneva: Geneva Centre for the Democratic Control of Armed Forces/International Security Sector Advisory Team: 2011), p. 18.

2 United Nations, *United Nations Peacekeeping Operations: Principles and Guidelines* (New York: United Nations, 2008), p. 27.

Geneva Centre for the Democratic Control of Armed Forces (DCAF)

Albrecht Schnabel; Vanessa Farr (Eds.)
Back to the Roots: Security Sector Reform and Development
There has now been more than a decade of conceptual work, policy development and operational activity in the field of security sector reform (SSR). To what extent has its original aim to support and facilitate development been met? The different contributions to this volume address this question, offering a range of insights on the theoretical and practical relevance of the security-development nexus in SSR. They examine claims of how and whether SSR effectively contributes to achieving both security and development objectives. In particular, the analyses presented in this volume provide a salutary lesson that development and security communities need to take each other's concerns into account when planning, implementing and evaluating their activities.
The book offers academics, policy-makers and practitioners within the development and security communities relevant lessons, suggestions and practical advice for approaching SSR as an instrument that serves both security and development objectives.
vol. , 2011, 376 pp., 39,90 €, br., ISBN-CH 978-3-643-80117-3

LIT Verlag Berlin – Münster – Wien – Zürich – London
Auslieferung Deutschland / Österreich / Schweiz: siehe Impressumsseite

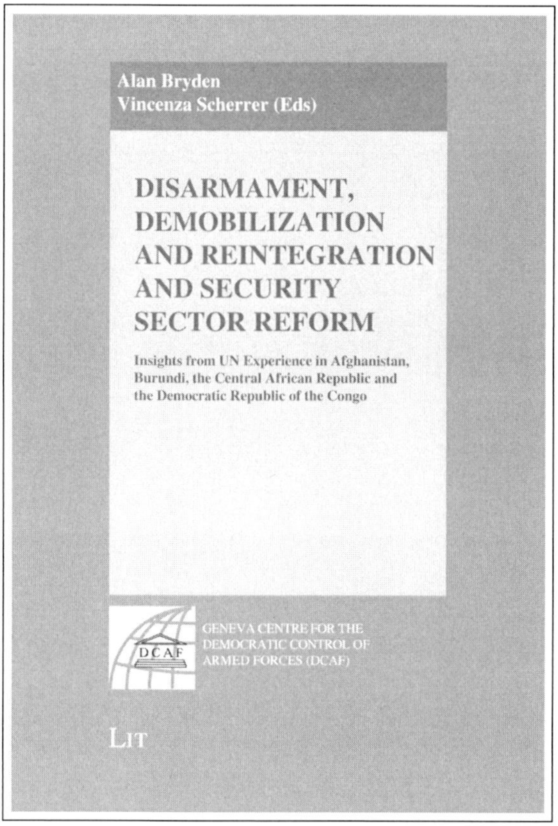

Alan Bryden; Vincenza Scherrer (Eds.)
Disarmament, Demobilization and Reintegration and Security Sector Reform
Insights from UN Experience in Afghanistan, Burundi, the Central African Republic and the Democratic Republic of the Congo
This volume sets out to break down these stove-pipes and identify positive associations between DDR and SSR. Drawing on case studies from selected post-conflict settings, it demonstrates the potential and reality of improved collaboration between both endeavours. Enhanced cooperation could avoid negative outcomes. These may include former- combatants dropping out of programmes, trust undermined in security institutions and the creation of security vacuums that jeopardise the safety of individuals and communities. A central claim of this volume is that programmes must be responsive to the needs and interests of different national actors. Without understanding the dynamic political processes that shape the origins, parameters and outcomes of both processes, DDR and SSR may address security deficits, but will be unfit to support sustainable transitions towards national recovery and development.
vol. , 2012, 232 pp., 29,90 €, br., ISBN-CH 978-3-643-80132-6

LIT Verlag Berlin – Münster – Wien – Zürich – London
Auslieferung Deutschland / Österreich / Schweiz: siehe Impressumsseite